RESOURCING RURAL MINISTRY

Published by
The Bible Reading Fellowship
15 The Chambers, Vineyard
Abingdon OX14 3FE
United Kingdom
Tel: +44 (0)1865 319700
Email: enquiries@brf.org.uk
Website: www.brf.org.uk
BRF is a Registered Charity

ISBN 978 0 85746 262 6

First published 2015
10 9 8 7 6 5 4 3 2 1 0
All rights reserved

Acknowledgements
Unless otherwise stated, scripture quotations are taken from The New Revised
Standard Version of the Bible, Anglicised edition, copyright © 1989, 1995 by the
Division of Christian Education of the National Council of the Churches of Christ
in the United States of America. Used by permission. All rights reserved.

Scripture quotations from the Contemporary English Version. New Testament
© American Bible Society 1991, 1992, 1995. Old Testament © American Bible
Society 1995. Anglicisations © British & Foreign Bible Society 1996. Used by
permission.

'The Bigger Picture' diagram from *Developing Healthy Churches* by Robert Warren,
published by Church House Publishing. © Robert Warren, 2012. Used by
permission. copyright@churchofengland.org.uk

Cover photos: Pauws99 / Thinkstock; Adrian Fortune / Thinkstock;
andresr / Getty Images

Every effort has been made to trace and contact copyright owners for material
used in this resource. We apologise for any inadvertent omissions or errors, and
would ask those concerned to contact us so that full acknowledgement can be
made in the future.

A catalogue record for this book is available from the British Library

Printed and bound by CPI Group (UK) Ltd, Croydon CR0 4YY

RESOURCING
RURAL
MINISTRY

PRACTICAL INSIGHTS FOR MISSION

Simon Martin

with Caroline Hewlett,
Rona Orme and Becky Payne

Edited by Jill Hopkinson

To all the unsung congregations and clergy who serve
so that the good news of Jesus Christ can contine to be
shared with all those who live in the countryside.

Acknowledgements

I am extremely grateful to Naomi Starkey and Lisa Cherrett and their colleagues at BRF, for their patience and skill, without which this book would not have been finished. My grateful thanks to Katrina Sealey, Elizabeth Clark and Jerry Marshall at the Arthur Rank Centre, who have greatly assisted in the preparation of the manuscript in more ways than they know.

The finishing touches were made to the text on the feast of Mary, Martha and Lazarus. The stories of their remarkable relationship with Jesus offer something of an allegory for the contemporary rural church. Here was Mary, who paid attention, listened and developed her discipleship; and Martha, who offered loving service and care to all. Then there was Lazarus, who was blessed to have new life through Christ our Lord. These attributes of loving service and care can be found in almost all rural churches. We perhaps need to pay more attention than we have before to deepening our relationship with God so that we can be open to new life.

About the authors

Simon Martin has been Training and Resources Officer at the Arthur Rank Centre (the churches' rural resources unit in Warwickshire) since 2005, having spent nearly 16 years working in general and theological education with the Church of Uganda, followed by five years of full-time lay ministry and local church training delivery in the UK. He has written a wide range of resources and training materials for rural churches, on subjects including mission, evangelism, Messy Church and discipleship. Simon is committed to developing the ministry of lay people within the rural church. He has previously published books on discipleship and small group leadership.

Revd Caroline Hewlett is Vicar of Swaledale with Arkengarthdale. This is a remote rural parish in the northern Yorkshire Dales, an area of tourism and hill sheep farming, with four churches over 250 square miles. Her work there includes a community conservation project in an ancient churchyard and experiments with Forest Church. She is a trustee of the Arthur Rank Centre and part of a team that runs a church presence at the Great Yorkshire Show. Before ordination, she worked with The Universities and Colleges Christian Fellowship, supporting Christian Unions in academic institutions across Yorkshire. Her curacy was in Leeds city centre, where she also acted as Chaplain to the Law Courts.

Jill Hopkinson is National Rural Officer for the Church of England, based at the Arthur Rank Centre. She is responsible for advice on rural and agricultural policy for the Archbishops' Council and provides training, support and consultancy for rural dioceses, clergy and congregations. She edits *Country Way* magazine and has written for and edited four previous books on rural mission and ministry. Jill regularly leads worship in the six-parish benefice where she lives, and co-leads Messy Church. She has a PhD in agricultural science and is an Honorary Lay Canon of Worcester Cathedral.

Rona Orme is the Children's Missioner in the Diocese of Peterborough. Passionate about working with children and families, she is the author of *Rural Children, Rural Church* (Church House Publishing, 2007), which came from her experience of working in rural parishes in Devon for nearly 25 years. She is a licensed Reader in the Church of England and now leads a weekly worship gathering for families in a primary school near Northampton. Her most recent books include *Creative Mission* and *More Creative Mission*, published by BRF.

Becky Payne, formerly an archaeologist, worked for several years at English Heritage. Between 2003 and 2010 she was Policy Officer in the Church Buildings Division of the Church of England. She is now a freelance consultant in sustaining historic places of worship. Recent projects have included creating a web-based resource on rural places of worship for the Arthur Rank Centre, updating a toolkit on developing churches for wider community use for the Diocese of Hereford, and work with the Plunkett Foundation on social enterprise. She provided the content for the book *Churches for Communities: Adapting Oxfordshire's churches for wider use*, published by the Oxfordshire Historic Churches Trust (2014).

Contents

Contents

Foreword

This book is a vital, timely and practical resource for rural mission and ministry. Contrary to the perception in some quarters, mission is flourishing in many rural communities and rural churches can be good at mission if they allow time and space for it to take place. Rural churches are at the forefront of the development of the ministry of lay people, shared ministry and fresh expressions. Rural church members are typically deeply involved in their communities and with local schools, and are often working ecumenically.

Yet there remain major challenges. As stipendiary clergy numbers fall, collaborative ministry and ecumenical working become essential. This in turn requires changes in leadership style, lay 'ownership' of mission, an openness to change, and a fresh look at how we use buildings, in order to sustain and develop an effective Christian presence in every community.

There are no quick answers but this book contains a remarkable range of resources to inspire, encourage and equip rural church members and leaders. The approach and content outlined are part of the developing Germinate programme of resources and training created by the Arthur Rank Centre (www.germinate.net).

Finally, I want to pay tribute to Simon Martin, who worked on this book before he fell seriously ill in 2014; to the other expert contributors—Caroline Hewlett, Rona Orme and Becky Payne; to my colleague Canon Dr Jill Hopkinson whose careful editing made this such a valuable and usable resource; and to BRF for their vision and patient support.

Jerry Marshall, CEO, The Arthur Rank Centre

Introduction

Jill Hopkinson

This is a book for people from any denomination, lay or ordained, with an interest in rural church mission and ministry. It draws together ideas, information and resources developed over several years by the Arthur Rank Centre (ARC). The book uses practical examples from several denominations to illustrate the key points and show the potential for local churches to be carriers of God's love to their rural communities.

The Arthur Rank Centre, the ecumenical resource centre for rural churches established in 1972, has long provided support, resources and ideas for use by rural congregations and communities. This book continues the work, developing a focus on the ministry of lay people, which will be so essential for the future of churches in rural areas.

Ministry, not just ministers

We believe passionately that Christian ministry is not the sole preserve of those who are ordained. This book is based on an underlying theological conviction that ministry is the responsibility and privilege of the whole body of Christ in any locality.

For some, perhaps many, in rural areas, convictions about lay ministry may be essentially pragmatic, arising from the observation that the number of clergy in rural areas has declined. This is particularly so where large numbers of churches have been brought together, and it holds true across different denominations and in a wide variety of rural contexts. So a growing commitment to ministry by the whole people of God may be driven by the recognition that 'we don't have our own minister any more' and the conclusion, 'so now we'll all have to muck in'.

However, it is increasingly recognised that there is a fundamental biblical, theological and ecclesiological affirmation of the involvement of everyone in ministry, regardless of financial constraints or the presence or absence of ordained clergy. This idea has many labels: the priesthood of all believers, the ministry of all the baptised, every-member ministry, lay ministry and the ministry of lay people. The case for the ministry of lay people is not argued here; nor do we delve into the various models by which ordained ministry continues to operate in such circumstances. We assume that, in rural churches, lay ministry is a given.

All the material in this book is for everyone involved with rural churches, including external training providers. In order to resource the ministry of lay people, clergy may first need to be resourced and assisted to develop new ways of working, acting as facilitators or *animateurs* for their congregations.[1]

However, not every rural church or group of churches welcomes the ministry of lay people. Traditional expectations often reinforce a model of church life in which clergy do the ministry and the congregation receive it. Both clergy and congregation can easily end up colluding with this approach. Alternatively, congregations may see themselves, at least, as 'helping out' or carrying out tasks delegated to them. In other places there is a real desire to develop a shared approach to mission and ministry, with a focus on teamwork and the development of the ministry of lay people.

For some, rural ministry will simply be shorthand for ministering in a rural situation and will be seen as not much different from forms of ministry elsewhere. This is not the case, as there are some very important characteristics of Christian ministry and mission in rural areas that are either absent from or much less prominent in the suburbs or cities.

The impact of rural situations

Rural churches and rural communities are different from those elsewhere. Small populations, the absence of public services, and travel distances and times all make a difference. Although many concepts and resources do not translate for use in rural churches, some do, others do with adaptation, and some initiatives and projects are ideally suited. There are also opportunities for ministry and mission that are not found in towns and cities.

While, overall, the culture of rural churches may be more conservative than in large towns and cities, the countryside is not a single homogeneous area. Every community and landscape area is different, and there is no single type of rural church, congregation or ministry. The examples, illustrations and resources in this book emerge from a very wide range of rural contexts. The issues facing people and the churches or chapels that serve them will be quite different in a string of isolated upland hamlets, a market town and a rural community that largely houses commuters.

Research carried out by the ARC[2] shows the impact of a rural location or background on the provision of training courses and the relevance of resources. Issues of concern include the content of courses and materials, which often does not fulfil the needs, whether practical or theoretical, of rural congregations. Some resources may have irrelevant content or make assumptions that are not relevant to the situations of small or isolated rural churches or communities. For example, a Methodist District promoted a discipleship programme but found that participation by their rural congregations dropped off sharply as all the stories and examples in the course were based on urban or suburban situations. Frequently, churches of all denominations provide training only in centralised locations, ignoring distance and difficulties of travel. However, training provided at a more local level may struggle to create a critical mass of participants.

Types of resourcing

There is a wide variety of materials highlighted in this book, accompanied by case studies to illustrate how the materials might be used. This approach is intended to act as a catalyst for you to try things in your own churches and communities, adapting as necessary. Many of the stories in this book, unless otherwise indicated, have either been published in the ARC's *Country Way* magazine or can also be found on our website. However, it has become increasingly obvious that equipping rural congregations takes more than designing or providing appropriate resources or training materials. It starts with preparing the congregation for involvement in all aspects of church and community life, and each part of this process points to areas where an ordained minister can have a unique and vital role.

Envisioning

This is the starting point—sharing the idea with congregation members. Envisioning will be a scary concept for many but exciting for others. It will involve exploring the theology of the whole people of God, the different gifts that people have and the skills that can be used for the kingdom of God. This might be done through a sermon series, special group meetings or services, a Lent or Bible study group, or time taken over a cup of tea after a service to get people talking. Consultation and listening are key parts of the process, as are learning from experiences elsewhere and allaying some of the fears. Robert Warren's material contained in *Developing Healthy Churches*[3] may be helpful.

Enabling

What gifts, skills and ideas are present in the congregations? Do some people want to explore vocations for service in the church, the local community or the world? Resources such as *Your Shape for God's Service*, prepared by the Diocese of Carlisle for use in small rural churches, help people explore their gifts and skills and their vocations to a wide range of roles and responsibilities. This resource helps people to understand the unique shape in which God has made them and how he might want to use them, which involves looking at:

- **S**piritual gifts (God's unique gifts to you)
- **H**eart's desire (what motivates and excites you)
- **A**bilities (your talents, knowledge and skills)
- **P**ersonality (your character, qualities and strengths)
- **E**xperiences (what you have gained from your life experiences)

The 'enabling' phase also requires some permission-giving, as well as encouragement to recognise that a broad range of gifts and skills is needed and that there will be many opportunities for them to be developed. It is important that roles that may appear to be trivial (for example, making refreshments) are valued and seen as an equally significant—indeed, vital—part of ministry.

Equipping

Equipping is about encouraging, providing training where needed, and offering ongoing support, mentoring and proper supervision. It should also include regular reviews of what is happening with both teams and individuals, depending on their task and role. This approach requires a significant investment of time and expertise that may well need to be drawn from several different people, not just the minister. However, one of the benefits of a multi-church group is that small numbers from each congregation may be brought together, even if the individuals work only in their own church rather than across the whole group.

Experience shows that growing ownership of lay ministry by rural congregations goes hand-in-hand with the development of appropriate mission within these same rural churches and the communities they serve.

Mission

What rural multi-church groups and individual churches and chapels have in their favour, among many things, is the potential to thrive. They offer a sense of rootedness and place of belonging in a changing context and in difficult social and world situations. The flipside of this is, of course, demonstrated by the reluctance of some members of rural congregations to travel to worship elsewhere. However, this rootedness, often shown in a commitment to the church building, offers a starting point for engagement and a foundation on which to extend and deepen relationships.

Rural churches can be good at mission. Rural congregations can have mission at their heart when the right conditions are created for that mission to start and be sustained. The key features that contribute to those conditions include the various roles of many congregation members who wear multiple 'hats' in a range of community activities and events; the fuzzy edges of many congregations; the experience of knowing and being known by everyone in rural communities (for good and for ill); and a culture of envisioning, enabling and equipping. These features are also a starting point for community engagement and a building block for extending and deepening relationships—personal, corporate and community. They form the basis for initiating and developing lay leadership, which then contributes to mission, ministry and evangelism.

One of the most important roles for churches in villages is to support the work of regular congregation members, where God has placed them in the world, to help them to carry faith with them in deed and word.

Many of the stories and examples in the following chapters are taken from situations where multiple churches are grouped together. This situation strongly influences the background to decisions that have been taken, resources and people that are available, and the location and timing of events.

One thing that emerges in many stories involving multiple rural churches is the necessity of working together. Partnership is essential and can be put into practice between neighbouring churches or groups of churches of the same denomination, or on an ecumenical basis, often in a market town or across a large geographical area. In some cases, partnership begins simply because one congregation alone cannot create sufficient critical mass to set up an event or activity. In other areas, it is more intentional or stems from a recognition of the reality that things are better done together.

How to use this book

This is not the first word in rural mission and ministry; nor will it be the last. It is intended as a guide to some of the main aspects of mission and ministry in rural communities, providing details of relevant resources and approaches, case studies and ideas. It is intended to be used in conjunction with the ARC website (www.germinate.net). It is relevant for members of rural congregations, lay church leaders, ordained ministers, training officers, advisers on vocation and selection, and senior staff.

This book has been written mostly by Simon Martin, as Training and Resources Officer for the ARC, over a period of two years between 2012 and the beginning of 2014. We are extremely grateful to Revd Caroline Hewlett, Rona Orme and Becky Payne for their significant contributions in writing the three chapters on worship, children and young people and church buildings.

Notes

1 For example, see David Heywood, *Reimagining Ministry* (SCM Press, 2011) or Robin Greenwood, *Being Church: The formation of Christian community* (SPCK, 2013).
2 Simon Martin, *Resourcing and Training for the Rural Church* (Arthur Rank Centre, 2011).
3 Robert Warren, *Developing Healthy Churches: Returning to the heart of mission and ministry* (Church House Publishing, 2012).

Mission in rural contexts

Simon Martin

When rural congregations discuss mission, it is often assumed that they mean attracting non-churchgoers to come to regular worship. While this remains important, the move from not attending church to a regular commitment may be a journey of many years. Most British citizens now have little knowledge of Christian basics, the Bible and church life. There is also a generation gap in many congregations, whether they are in rural areas or not. So this chapter focuses on how Christian values and principles are expressed by rural congregations and experienced in wider society.

Those who attend church are often deeply involved in different aspects of rural community life, providing leadership, inspiration and encouragement. It would be possible to identify a wide range of organisations that are supported, organised and led by members of rural congregations. As an example, in one Warwickshire village the carnival, educational foundation, school governors, footpath group, environment group, Neighbourhood Watch, parish council, Women's Institute, Scout groups and Brownies—to name but ten activities—would not function without the involvement of members of the local churches. Similar lists could no doubt be produced for most rural communities. In such places, this deep involvement and activity makes the boundaries between congregation and community very blurred.

In some places, church and community will be so deeply integrated that they are almost synonymous with each other;

elsewhere there may be good overlaps and links, and in other places there may be a complete disconnection between congregation and community, with the church simply being yet another group existing only for itself.

An Anglican curate talks of visits made during a study trip in the north-east of England.

> The last visit we made was to the conversion of a small workhouse in a remote village. Here, a committed parish priest had worked for years, building connections and networks of investors, taking on a small row of shops, funding some affordable housing, and now a beautiful community centre, which housed the library, a tourist information centre, meeting rooms, and offices available for rent. And I reflected on the challenge— to make it clear why Christians try to do this sort of thing, building and supporting communities—because if it isn't to share 'the knowledge and love of God and of His Son Jesus Christ our Lord', then why do we do it?

Motivation

Why do Christians get involved in rural community events and organisations? *Faith in Rural Communities*[1] looked at the contributions of rural church congregations to the social capital and vibrancy of rural communities. This research explored the reasons why Christians got involved in community life.

* Some were clear about the contribution they brought as a person of faith. Regular prayer and worship provided the basis for right living, care for others, trusting relationships and a willingness to forgive and accept forgiveness. All these were vital ingredients in establishing healthy communities, and they derived from paying attention to the spiritual dimension of life.

21

- Others expressed a clear motivational link between faith and action. Their behaviour was a practical and visible outworking, in private and public life, of their personal faith. People of faith wanted to show the 'love, concern and acceptance that the church ought to show'.[2]
- Others identified a social obligation, encouraged by a shortage of willing volunteers.
- The idea of an active faith in the community set the context for the outworking of faith—as a contributor to social well-being, both economic and community based, rather than being solely concerned for the building up of the church.
- Others focused on voluntary and community activity, with a strong feeling that organisations like the church need to be involved to bring people together and make things happen.
- There were some who found it hard to identify the source of their motivation: 'This is just part of life,' they suggested.[3]
- Many revealed overlapping motivations, plus 'issues of justice, which as Christians we really ought to be fighting for, all the time'.[4]

Similar research[5] into the social involvement of local churches in the Oxford area revealed that a number of people outside the church, themselves engaged in community activities, often had a clearer sense of what motivated churchgoers to get involved than the churchgoers themselves. It was 'because they have faith', and the people outside the church were neither surprised nor put off by this.

Research by the Institute of Volunteering Research[6] suggests that, along with age, gender and employment status, faith is an important factor in leading some to volunteer. In other research on volunteering in rural Scotland,[7] a similar pattern emerged, showing a much higher level of voluntary activity than in urban areas. Churchgoing is identified as one of four key markers for volunteering and community involvement. Of course, there are many people who make vital contributions to their rural communities who do not share the faith of churchgoers. Yet it is important to remember that, in many cases, the networks and organisations that contribute to rural community vibrancy are shared by both non-churchgoers and people of faith together.

Nevertheless, volunteers who are Christians can, and often do, add a distinctive presence and contribution to their community and activities. These added values can be either indirect, through community projects, events, organisations and presence, or direct, through church projects and outreach activities. Those who are involved in their local church can help bring 'salt, light and yeast' to the heart of rural community life (see Matthew 5:13–16; Luke 13:20–21). So, at the very least, congregation members need to be equipped to be effective Christians where God has placed them in the world. This equipping is particularly important for those members of rural congregations who are unable or unwilling to acknowledge the importance of their faith in what they do. Some congregation members will be surprised to know that they are carrying out mission in their everyday lives, in an unconscious and unintentional way.

It is a very valuable exercise to identify the groups and activities in which congregation members take part, and the professional roles or areas of responsibility that they hold. It is then important to continue to pray for these groups, activities and roles on a regular basis, as part of public worship.

Where does mission take place?

This question is partially answered by the experience of a rector from a geographically dispersed rural multi-parish benefice in the West Midlands.

> I recognise that many of our core parishioners are fully part of the daily mission of the church just by being so involved in their communities: meals on wheels, visiting the sick or housebound, local transport rota, volunteer-working in the post office, reading assistance in the primary school, after-school clubs, the local environmental group, running a Fairtrade stall. I think telling them to get explicitly involved in some centrally defined version of mission will draw them away from this, and give them the message that official church stuff is more important than what they are already doing. I would rather reinforce these things done locally than adopt external programmes, even when provided by [the diocese]. Of course, the trick is to help them see that what they are already doing is part of the overall mission of the local church. That isn't so easy!

Volunteering within the community, while not the same as intentional mission, may well be closely linked to it, since many of the activities are indeed firmly encompassed within a broad understanding of mission that includes loving service, pastoral care and evangelism. Additionally, in many cases the motivation of the individuals is derived from either their personal faith or what they believe is expected of the local church and Christians as a whole.

Robert Warren helpfully outlines a threefold pattern for the way in which local churches and their members engage in mission.[8]

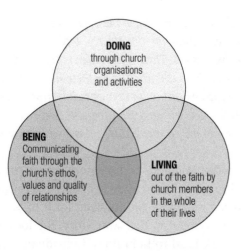

FIG: 'THE BIGGER PICTURE' FROM *DEVELOPING HEALTHY CHURCHES* BY
ROBERT WARREN

This highlights some significant issues regarding mission in
the local rural church:

- There are recognisable differences between explicit (Doing)
  and implicit (Living and Being) engagement.
- Formal, explicit church events and activities (Doing)
  are important, but may be of limited relevance for small
  congregations, large numbers of churches grouped
  together and dispersed communities (like many in rural
  situations).
- The informal contributions of the lives (Living) and
  relationships (Being) of churchgoers are extremely significant for effective mission.

Warren explains:

> *Smaller, often rural, churches may be richly involved in*
> *Christian mission without setting up a single organisation…*

*Not only do they not have the resources to run things such as luncheon clubs for the elderly, but it would be counter-productive to do so. Their role, rather, is to join with the village groups running such activities. In these situations the church is not called to be **light** (with its own visible structures) but rather **leaven** (hidden within local activities). However, this call to be leaven is not just 'a nice picture', it is a serious piece of work.[9]*

As in the West Midlands rector's story earlier, the church does not need to organise, or even sanction, everything in which local church members get involved for it to be real mission. But, again as noted in the same story, the local church may have to work hard to help these individuals recognise their activities as real mission and, just as importantly, to affirm and support them in what they do. In fact, many local churches themselves may fail to recognise the individuals' engagement as mission. This is illustrated by the common situation where congregation members are prayed for in relation to their explicit church activities (for example, children's activity leaders, church officers, musicians) but not for their engagements outside the church building, such as their work or voluntary activities. Among other things, this sends a subliminal message that activities outside church are not so important to the life, ministry and mission of the local church.

Why does this happen? From the perspective of the church, the primary reason is likely to be that habit, tradition or expectation limits the recognition of 'mission' to what the church has explicitly set up or sanctioned. There is a widespread tendency to see a church only in organisational terms, through its internal or external activities or events. Churches are often more focused on providing or creating mission than on recognising it and affirming it where it is already taking place. There are theological elements that lie behind such attitudes—not least a threefold loss:

- loss of vision that this is God's mission
- loss of recognition that, in mission, God's people are not so much sent out from the church as called to join where God is already present and active
- loss of understanding of the dimensions of God's kingdom —overlapping with all of creation, and recognisable everywhere that divine norms and priorities are evident, regardless of who is actually responsible

From the perspective of individual churchgoers engaging in these missional situations, the reasons probably also revolve around habit, tradition and expectation.

- If congregation members have not had their activities recognised and affirmed as mission by the church, they are unlikely to appreciate that these are an integral and vital part of the mission of their local church.
- Likewise, if the different aspects of mission, whole-life faith and discipleship have not been explored as part of worship or in small groups, congregation members are unlikely to see what they do as God's work or as an outworking of their own faith.

For some rural churches there is an important gap to be bridged from church-centred perceptions of mission to recognition, affirmation and support for implicit mission. Bridging this gap would encourage both the church and the individuals involved. It might also help individuals to think through the purposes of their involvement and, as a result, be more intentional regarding mission. For example, intentional involvement might encourage a greater role in hospitality, overt prayer for those in need or reconciliation.

This bridging could be started by encouraging all church members to participate in learning about the Five Marks of Mission[10] and about whole-life faith and discipleship. Perhaps key to this process is the provision of an opportunity for ordinary church members to recognise their current activities as valued by the church and as a genuine part of God's activity.

Stories about other people and congregations engaged in implicit mission will help to model what being a missional congregation is all about. This is one step removed from having to reflect directly on personal experience, which can be uncomfortable for some. Permanent changes of attitude, by individuals and by a congregation as a whole, generally come only through encouraging people to ask questions and discuss all aspects of mission with each other. Small, informal groups are usually the best context for this, and there are good materials (detailed towards the end of this chapter) that can catalyse questions and discussions about mission.

What is the rural church good at?

The Five Marks of Mission are:

- to proclaim the good news of the kingdom: **tell**
- to teach, baptise and nurture new believers: **teach**
- to respond to human need by loving service: **tend**
- to seek to transform the unjust structures of society, challenge violence of every kind, and pursue peace and reconciliation: **transform**

- to strive to safeguard the integrity of creation, and sustain and renew the life of the earth: **treasure**

There are two differing views about rural churches and mission. The first view sees only small congregations, elderly worshippers, old and deteriorating buildings, growing financial burdens and decreasing numbers of ordained clergy caring for increasing numbers of churches. It concludes that rural churches are poorly placed to engage in explicit, organised, effective mission. The second view recognises that these are very real issues but affirms that the rural church is actually good at mission—or it can be if it makes use of the talents and opportunities that are already present.

Mission is possible in the countryside, where there is recognition of the skills and resources actually available— people, experience, buildings, land, schools and even whole communities. This mission is often implicit and without formal church organisation; at least, it starts as such. Mission in the countryside is primarily about 'living' and 'being' first and foremost, with 'doing' as the third part of the mix. Showing and sharing what mission activity looks like can attract those on the edge of or outside the worshipping community.

Looking at the Five Marks summarising the mission of the church, we can draw several general conclusions about mission in rural churches.

- Rural churches are probably best at *tending*—responding to human need by loving service.
- There has been good work done in many rural churches in *teaching*, especially in terms of baptising and nurturing new believers, often in quite low-key and localised ways. Perhaps less successful is the involvement in continuing

faith development for those with lengthier experiences of faith.

- Some rural churches have engaged creatively and meaning-fully with *treasuring*—striving to safeguard the integrity of creation, often linked with agricultural issues and climate change.
- While there are some great rural examples of *telling* the good news of the kingdom and seeking to *transform* the unjust structures of society, these marks can be more challenging for many rural churches, especially (but not exclusively) the very small ones.

Knowing your context

Michael Langrish, writing in *Changing Rural Life*,[11] stresses that a church should be firmly rooted in the particular and the local, literally embodying God's mission and the scriptural story in specific places.

In her book *The Word in Place*, Louise Lawrence describes research she undertook with five different groups of people: residents of a rural village, inner-city residents, those living in a fishing village, people who are deaf, and ordained clergy. All were invited to read and reflect on the same scriptural passage. She notes:

> *While the same biblical stories were encountered by each group, the wisdom drawn from these texts in the respective contexts was also very different... The rural village group... consisted of both church attendees and non-attendees. The exchange between these individuals throughout the process brought greater mutual understanding.*[12]

From such reflections several important conclusions can be drawn.

- Each local church needs to learn to describe and understand its cultural context.
- This context is not just the physical locality but includes the ethos, patterns and values of society.
- The local church and its members do not know everything about their own community; learning about their context will include listening to people outside the church.
- Learning about its context may not be an easy exercise for the local church. Many rural communities are in a state of flux, and their dynamics are often deep and unspoken. Learning is best done from inside a rural community, as Langrish recognises: 'many rural congregations are at the core of the local social fabric', which provides vital inside knowledge.

Less explicitly, we can also conclude that the church has to know itself, its strengths and weaknesses, and the threats and opportunities it faces. It is also important that rural churches perceive themselves accurately. As the saying goes, 'a tangerine is not a failed orange'! This illustrates the often neglected truth that small rural churches are not failed larger ones. It serves as an important reminder that the local context is of crucial importance for appropriate and successful mission. It also serves to highlight that this difference of context means that small rural churches cannot, and should not, attempt to mimic all the activities, programmes and approaches of their larger suburban counterparts.

Mission Action Planning (MAP) is being used increasingly to help churches understand their context, the opportunities it presents and the extent of their own resources. It is essentially a tool to prepare local churches for structured and intentional mission as part of larger initiatives in mission run by a diocese or district. Although the preparation work for MAP may seem daunting, especially for very small congregations, there are considerable benefits for rural churches and groups of rural churches in using MAP, especially when they work together. These include:

- the ability to review current church activities honestly and evaluate their suitability for the congregation and wider community
- assisting congregations to identify opportunities, start new initiatives (and stop others) and understand the resources available
- improve communication within the congregation and wider community
- provide a focus to help churches think about and plan for the future

From the perspective of many rural churches, though, MAP can have some drawbacks.

- It is not particularly well-suited to small churches with few active members who choose to work by themselves, and it does not always take into consideration that the MAP may be undertaken by a group of churches with shared ordained leadership.
- It can overlook the significance and extent of the implicit mission already being done by church members, which, as we have already seen, is one of the strengths of many rural churches.

- It can neglect the important element of partnership (with other churches as well as non-religious organisations and local groups) that is crucial for success or even survival in many rural communities.

The Arthur Rank Centre (ARC) has produced a bespoke toolkit to help any rural church or group of churches to make the most of their opportunities and strengths and to address some of their weaknesses. *Equipping for Rural Mission* (available at www.germinate.net/go/profiling) is a simple, flexible, free resource designed to be used by a small church or group of churches over a few sessions. The toolkit takes you through a straightforward process which includes:

- appreciating your church(es)—accurately assessing your own resources, including the gifts and skills of the congregation(s)
- discovering and recognising what you are already doing
- investigating and understanding what your communities are like and discovering what they think and expect
- looking at what is already being done by others, and how you might join in, or investigating how you might start something new in partnership with others
- working out what you are realistically able to do and what is most appropriate in engaging with your communities
- reflecting and making decisions about what might be started and what might need to be stopped

A churchwarden from one group of rural parishes in Derbyshire who used this toolkit reported:

It wasn't like anything we'd ever used before. To start with, we actually had to get out and do some finding out and talking to people instead of just sitting in meetings listening to experts talking! We discovered some very interesting things about our villages that we hadn't realised, especially about what people thought of the church (which wasn't always encouraging). But what was really encouraging was learning about all the little things that church folk have been doing in their own patches.

We've had our feedback and reflection day and we've decided where we can start doing some new things together; we've got more gifts and better skills than most of us realised. So we want to start a Messy Church, to be run between four of our six churches, and we hope to start fortnightly second-hand or local produce stalls alongside a children's activity, coffee and bacon baps in [the biggest village]. It has been harder realising that we might need to stop some activities so that we can channel our energy into similar things being done better by others.

The power of story

Stories are as important to people in the church as elsewhere. Rural congregations and their leaders can be greatly encouraged by hearing stories of how people like them have done things elsewhere. There are many ways in which stories can be shared. When this happens, there are often numerous nodding heads and murmurs of recognition. What is surprising, though, is that such apparently widespread recognition seldom finds its way into the resourcing of local churches. Both research and experience reveal that the major reason for this is lack of knowledge about where good stories can be found, often compounded by a lack of avenues to distribute or share helpful stories.

Swap shop

Revd Claire Lording talks about the Ludlow Deanery Swap Shop, which emerged from a deanery discussion about rural mission. They asked the question, 'How do we, as church, engage with our rural communities in a meaningful way?'

We realised that we all approached this task in different ways and that within the deanery there was a wealth of experience and expertise. So we agreed to put on an event that would enable every parish of the deanery to come together to celebrate what they do in their context and to share their good practice with the rest of the deanery. The aim was to affirm parishes in what they already do, to encourage them to see what other parishes were doing, and to enable mutual learning.

Who did we want to invite and involve? Our diocese has a clear strategy for promoting Mission Action Planning and wants to enable PCCs to be part of this process, so that they, along with the whole church community and the wider community, can think about what their hopes are for the future, and how their priorities can best reflect God's priorities. So early on it was agreed that the Swap Shop would primarily be for PCC members, the idea being that they could not only come along and share what they do but could learn from the experiences of other PCCs and parishes, which would hopefully feed into their own Mission Action Planning. The Swap Shop would also provide an opportunity for parishes to evaluate how their activity corresponded with the Marks of Mission.

The day also provided a good opportunity for the deanery to learn together, and a small number of workshops were organised. The workshops looked at different aspects of mission, including exploring the talents to be found in the parishes, and looking at mission with young people.

At the Swap Shop itself, the hall buzzed with activity and conversation the whole day long. Many of the PCCs from the deanery had gone to a lot of trouble to be involved and there was a real sense of pride in what they were offering to the rest of the deanery. Among all the laptops, display boards of every size, photos and hands-on resources, offerings included a Traidcraft stall, 'Faith in the Pub', coffee mornings in various styles (including fresh bacon rolls on market day), welcome packs, adult Christian learning, Mothers' Union, a parents' and toddlers' group, Messy Church, the 'Off the Street' youth club, a link with Maramba in Tanzania, links with campers on holiday, family services, Godly Play, music and prayer, links with a local prison craft club, and Caring for God's Acre.[13]

The Swap Shop achieved its objective, in that it brought the deanery together to celebrate all that we do and all that we are. It also encouraged and supported the people and parishes of the deanery in working together to share God's kingdom with all. Many of those who came to the Swap Shop left with notebooks and heads full of ideas that they wanted to try out in their parishes. There was definitely a buzz about mission that morning and we hope that this will continue in the parishes of the deanery.

Other ways of sharing stories

Not every rural PCC or group of rural churches has opportunities to share face-to-face in this way, and, when such swapping of stories and ideas does take place, it tends to be within a relatively limited geographical area or a related group, such as a single Anglican deanery. On top of this, if we are honest, there is little face-to-face sharing of stories across denominational boundaries.

Nevertheless, there are ways to encounter examples of good practice elsewhere, such as through denominational or Churches Together publications, web-based collections of stories or online forums.

Country Way magazine

Prominent among these publications is the magazine *Country Way*, produced by the ARC. Every issue is replete with good stories from rural congregations across the country, in numerous contexts and from a variety of denominations and traditions.

A retired teacher in Yorkshire writes of how she has been encouraged to 'help get a few things going' having discovered *Country Way*.

I read about a Harvest Supper and shared the story with a few others in the chapel, and we decided that we'd try to organise one. The whole congregation and lots of others in the village got stuck in; local farmers and the shopkeeper provided good food; we got a (clean) barn for nothing; we roped in any 'local talent' we had for entertainment. On the night we had a Harvest Thanksgiving service with the local brass band in the barn, followed by a supper accompanied by a talent show, to which we got nearly 250 people—which is most of the village! Next on the list is a church-organised Big Cream Tea (again with a brass band—we are from Yorkshire, after all) and an outdoor service afterwards. This idea was also sparked by an article in *Country Way*. Maybe we can break the 300 mark if we can get visitors from outside to come as well.

Rural stories online

The ARC has a growing collection of stories focused on explicit mission: *Stories of Rural Hope*. The online 'Library of Rural Good Practice' contains pieces that provide greater depth and more detail. A significant proportion of the content focuses on community-based mission and evangelism, often also involving discipleship and nurture. Quite a few of these examples of good practice combine a story with discussion and evaluation of a particular resource, tool or approach from the rural perspective.

A Ministry Area Leader from the Church in Wales shares how she benefited from an online evaluation from the ARC.

> We've got eleven tiny churches in the outlying villages and bigger 'hub' churches in our two small towns. We're going to be learning to work together, and I'm looking seriously at ways of using the positive side of being small to encourage and develop all the church members. In particular we need something that helps small churches to be realistic about mission and ministry. Your resource evaluating the Scottish Episcopal Church's 'Welcoming Small Congregations' is really helpful as it shows that there is something already out there that others have used, which works—and our situations in rural Wales and rural Scotland aren't so different. So we've got their book of stories, which tells things as they really are, and, best of all, you've pointed out where we can get workbook material to download for ourselves. I'm planning to use this with the full Ministry Area Team when it is properly functioning.

It is important to note how such stories are best used. They are not intended to be slavishly copied. As discussed earlier, context is vital and no two rural churches or communities are identical. The stories can inspire, encourage and enthuse; they can be catalysts or stepping-stones for trying something new in your own location with judicious tweaking and a little Spirit-anointed imagination.

With the growing availability of free and easy-to-use multimedia tools on the web, increasing numbers of people are creating and sharing video clips and audio files online. Some of these are formal parts of larger web-based resources, good examples being CPAS and Fresh Expressions, and some of the material is specifically rural.

Interactive sharing of stories

It is also worth considering whether it might be helpful to share things that are being done in your own churches with others. There are a number of locations where you can share stories of rural mission or ministry. For some, like the ARC publications and web-based libraries already mentioned, you can make contact and send in material or ideas; these will then be made widely available in the most suitable way.

There are other web forums where you can add your own stories, ask questions or introduce a topic of conversation, open your material up for comments from other rural church practitioners, and benefit from others who have done the same. Many of these use some form of social media, usually a Facebook page or group or a blog. Some Facebook groups worth looking at include 'Renewing the Rural Church', 'Arthur Rank Centre', 'Country Way', 'Who Let The Dads Out?' and 'Messy Church—BRF'.

The following resources may be helpful.

- *Country Way*:
  www.countryway.org.uk
- Resources for rural communities:
  www.germinate.net/go/communities
- Library of Rural Good Practice:
  www.germinate.net/go/casestudies
- Equipping for rural mission toolkit:
  www.germinate.net/go/profiling
- Stories of rural HOPE:
  www.germinate.net/go/hopestories
- ARC on Facebook:
  www.facebook.com/arthurrankcentre

Notes

1 *Faith in Rural Communities: Contributions of social capital to community vibrancy* (ACORA, 2006). www.germinate.net/go/faithinruralcommunities

2 Ibid. p. 44

3 Ibid. p. 45

4 Ibid. p. 45

5 'Building better neighbourhoods: the contribution of faith communities to Oxordshire life' (2010): https://curve.coventry.ac.uk/open/items/32e0943c-358f-aed4-b5ba-b65edb591304/1

6 'Helping out: a national survey of volunteering and charitable giving', Office of the Third Sector in the Cabinet Office (2007), pp. 19–20: www.ivr.org.uk/images/stories/Institute-of-Volunteering-Research/Migrated-Resources/Documents/H/OTS_Helping_Out.pdf

7 Mike Woolvin and Alasdair Rutherford, 'Volunteering and public service reform in rural Scotland', Scottish Rural Policy Centre (2013), p. 5: www.volunteerscotland.net/media/235107/volunteering_and_public_service_reform.pdf

8 'The Bigger Picture' diagram, Robert Warren, *Developing Healthy Churches: Returning to the heart of mission and ministry* (Church House Publishing, 2012), p. 122

9 Warren, *Developing Healthy Churches*, p. 123

10 For more information on the Five Marks of Mission, see www.anglicancommunion.org/identity/marks-of-mission.aspx

11 Michael Langrish, 'Dynamics of Community' in J.M. Martineau, L.J. Francis and P. Francis (eds), *Changing Rural Life: A Christian response to key rural issues* (Canterbury Press, 2004), pp. 21–43

12 Louise J. Lawrence, *The Word in Place: Reading the New Testament in contemporary contexts* (SPCK, 2009), p. 136

13 For more information, see www.caringforgodsacre.org.uk

Multi-church ministry

Jill Hopkinson

Multi-church ministry in its various forms is a much-used strategy for managing the organisation of churches and the deployment of clergy. Almost all denominations with a presence in the countryside use this approach; indeed, the Methodist circuit system is predicated on ministers relating to more than one church across one or more communities. Multi-church groups are now an integral part of the Church of England in the countryside, with smaller numbers of churches from the United Reformed Church and Baptist Church also operating in groups. Increasingly, multi-church structures are found in urban and suburban locations too, although they have been present in rural communities for many decades.

One of the biggest factors in rural ministry is the number of churches within a grouping. Anglican multi-church groups often have between three and seven churches, with larger groups of churches (eleven or more) becoming increasingly common. Across the denominations, common numbers now range from five to 14 churches under the care of one or more ministers. The largest multi-church group in the Church of England comprises 25 churches. There are 84 churches, with twelve ministers, in the Shropshire and Marches Methodist Circuit. The distance and travel time between different communities and churches can be long. Many multi-church groupings can cover hundreds of square miles, with tens of miles between each church. Even where churches are closer together, a round trip of 25 miles would not be uncommon between services in different churches.

There remains a common perception among congregations, communities and, to a certain extent, clergy, that even up to the mid-20th century there was one minister for every church and, as a result, attendance at church was much higher. For the Church of England, where this view is a particular problem, with the exception of the 12th and 13th centuries (when there was indeed one priest for every church in every settlement) and the latter part of the 19th century, clergy numbers have never been high enough to attain this ratio.[1] When Revd Robert Hawker reintroduced the idea of the harvest festival in Cornwall in the 1840s, he had charge of three parishes.

Multi-church ministry brings with it a great many joys and opportunities, in working with different communities and congregations. It also has its own tensions and complications and can be stressful for lay and ordained alike. We know that it is possible for some churches in rural multi-church groups to grow and to do so consistently over several years.[2] We also know that many rural congregations have reduced in size and others maintain regular numbers attending. This chapter tries to address some of the key issues specific to multi-church ministry that are not covered in other chapters. It also takes a pragmatic approach. Despite recent research findings on church growth,[3] multi-church structures will remain in place through both intention and necessity.

The realities of multi-church ministry

When there are two or three churches in a group, the argument could be strongly made that the minister can still be expected to do most things, especially those with any spiritual content. It is assumed to be perfectly possible for one person to take three or more services on a Sunday, carry out all pastoral work, take funerals, weddings and baptisms, nurture new believers and run activities for children and young people. However, in reality, when the number of churches in a group increases to two or more, change has to take place, as it is impossible for one person to do it all (as is also, in fact, the case in a single church with a single minister). The danger is that the minister and congregations collude to ensure that the old model remains or that the minister feels so isolated or without help that they continue to try to do it all. The tragedy has been that in some places, without sufficient involvement from the congregation or appropriate invitation to be involved, the activity has been cut back drastically so that the minister can still do it all— just less of it in each place. Isolation, overwork, stress and sometimes breakdown are the result.

The active involvement and leadership of lay people, with clergy offering a role of oversight, will increasingly become the norm. This, of course, has been the experience of both the Methodist Church and the United Reformed Church for some time. In multi-church groups the ministry of lay people will have even greater importance than it does already, with collaboration between clergy and congregations, congregations and communities, and with different churches and denominations, an essential part of the future. The ministerial role will still involve all the important aspects of leading worship, pastoral care and mission, but it will also involve sharing those roles and envisioning, enabling and equipping others to do the same.

Aside from the imperative produced by logic and circumstance, scripture offers some pointers for sharing this work of the kingdom with others. The image of the body of Christ is used in several places in the New Testament, including Ephesians 4:11–13; Romans 12:4–8 and 1 Corinthians 12:12–28 ('the body does not consist of one member but of many', v. 14). All parts of the body are needed, those parts are diverse, there is no hierarchy and there are no passengers. To quote W.J. Carter, 'the church is the sum of its members' gifts';[4] these gifts should not be distinguished in value, as all are both necessary and important, regardless of whether the community or individual sees them as such.

Working out how to help people use their gifts, as opposed to finding people to fulfil particular tasks, is the challenge for all clergy in multi-church situations. While there can be resistance from some parts of congregations to increased lay ministry and shared leadership, there is also necessity—and not just because of the pragmatic recognition that clergy can no longer do it all. The development of the ministry of lay people is necessary because this is what God wants the church to be like. In the words of Hans-Reudi Weber, 'The laity are not helpers of the clergy so that the clergy can do their job, but the clergy are the helpers of the whole people of God, so that the laity can be the Church.'[5]

Commonly, groups of churches are thought of as being organised around one or more ministers rather than as churches present in different communities for the benefit of the people, which are served by the same minister or ministers. This misperception in the minds of most people belies the true purpose of multi-church groups, which is to facilitate worship and mission.

There is often tension between the needs and opportunities within an individual church and its wider community, and the benefits that can be drawn from being part of a larger group of churches. Several churches working together can create a critical mass of volunteers and participants in order to make it feasible to run a seekers' course, special event or children's activity. However, due to the nature of rural communities, friendships, networks and relationships are often at their strongest at the most local level and this is the place where outreach and mission can be most effective.

In some multi-church groups, the shared minister may be the only factor that each church or community has in common. Circuits, benefices and teams can represent ecclesiastical boundaries that have little meaning to those outside the church and may bring together communities that have no previous connection or even have enmity between them. Not every church congregation may be willing to collaborate with other churches in the group (including ecumenically) and not everyone will see the potential benefits of doing this. Although geography and distance can play a part in the reluctance to work with others in the multi-church group, there can be a strong desire to remain independent and retain an individual approach to worship and community life.

Ministers who have attempted to bring disparate churches together often reflect that the process was problematic, complex, time-consuming and long. One Anglican priest commented that his predecessor had 'worked extremely hard over several years telling the parishes "we need to work together"', and that eventually this need had been recognised. The process had included the development and encouragement of shared services, starting with fifth Sundays, congregations visiting other churches for worship and social events, and collective quiet days. In ten years the group had progressed from having one priest trying to keep things going by themselves, to having both formal and informal structures that supported the ministry and mission of many other people. Other ministers report that it can take three to four years from the formation of a new group for it to start to feel as if it is functioning as a group rather than as individual churches.

One large Anglican multi-parish benefice worked hard to bring together the disparate church congregations. They used a questionnaire to ask congregation members what they wanted and what their aspirations were for the group. Five key areas were identified and a working group was set up for each one. The five areas were:

- children and young people
- growth and learning
- pastoral care and service to the community
- resources (and administration)
- worship

Each working group had a representative from most of the PCCs, so most churches were represented. Special events and new initiatives could therefore be developed and 'owned' across the whole benefice. These working groups have also driven mission, setting priorities and making sure things are done. The incumbent was a member of each working group but did not chair them; the incumbent also delegated the chairing of each PCC to the lay vice-chair.

In numerous multi-church groups, joint services and events have been instrumental in starting joint working between different churches, whether of the same denomination or ecumenically. However, there will always be some people who will not get involved in anything outside their local church or community. Where an effort had been made to continue and build on joint services and events, in spite of some reluctance, there was often a better understanding of the strengths and weaknesses of each church, along with an appreciation that some events and services were better done in one location, targeted at a particular community or done as a whole group of churches.

Nevertheless, serious tensions can arise over the need to:

- bring different churches together to create a critical mass for activities, training or events.
- focus on the local congregation and community as, often, the most effective place for building relationships.

The Methodist Circuit

Constitution Practice and Discipline (CPD) of the Methodist Church defines a circuit in the following way.

The circuit is the primary unit in which local churches express and experience their interconnection in the body of Christ, for purposes of mission, mutual encouragement and help. It is in the circuit that presbyters, deacons and probationers are stationed and local preachers are trained and admitted and exercise their calling. The purposes of the circuit include the effective deployment of the resources of ministry, which include people, property and finance, as they relate to the Methodist churches in the circuit, to churches of other denominations and to participation in the life of the communities served by the circuit, including local schools and colleges, and in ecumenical work in the area including, where appropriate, the support of ecumenical Housing Associations.[6]

In practice, this means that the circuit provides the finance for ministry across the whole circuit, as most churches would struggle to 'pay' for a minister on their own. The decisions are made by the circuit meeting, which comprises the ordained ministers, lay staff, the circuit stewards and one or more representatives from each church, with representation depending on the number of churches in the circuit.

Circuits are responsible for the stationing process (the appointment of presbyters and deacons for each circuit), the upkeep of manses, and the administration of any circuit money held in the 'advance fund'. The 'advance fund' is usually money raised from the sale of buildings, although it may be from other sources, and is held at circuit level. This money is available for churches by application and is usually used to enhance the mission of a church, for ministry that is linked to mission (such as a youth worker) or for schemes to transform properties. Each circuit will have its own criteria for how such funds can be used, which also vary significantly in amount between different circuits. The policy and approach for mission may well be decided by the circuit, especially where a project has application across the whole circuit. Each church has a church council who are also the managing trustees of the building. Local churches are responsible for mission in their own communities but can also request help from the wider circuit.

There are good examples of individual churches within a circuit deciding to work together. For example, a small circuit of four churches in rural North Yorkshire has developed shared worship, particularly during Holy Week and Easter. They work together to provide a regular Messy Church in one of the villages and are now very used to sharing ideas, personnel, events and services.

Methodism also benefits from the well-established and supported ministry of lay people, through roles such as local preacher, worship leader or pastoral visitor. The ministry of lay people is well accepted and expected, with lay-led services of the word an integral part of the cycle of worship throughout the year. Both local preachers and worship leaders contribute significantly to the quarterly circuit plan for worship.

If the membership of a Methodist church falls below six, or if the congregation has problems filling the required appointments to the church council, such as treasurer or stewards, then it becomes a 'class' of another church. The larger church takes over the finance and administration of the smaller one and the local members can be freed for mission in their community. In the past, this has been seen as a way of subverting the church council with the aim of closing the building; however, the support given to the small worshipping congregation can enable it to make a positive difference, in a way that it was not able to before.

Becoming a class

Eggborough Methodist Church in North Yorkshire was a small congregation with falling numbers, and the building was vulnerable to closure. However, the circuit could see that there was still potential in this congregation, not least because they were the only church in the village, so they became a class of Brayton Methodist Church.

Regular worship moved from Sundays to Thursdays, taking place before a community coffee morning that was well supported. Once overall responsibility had been removed from the congregation, one or two people decided to be received into membership and share the task of building up the church community. The circuit also provided a working party to clear the church garden, which is now cared for locally and has become another community space, appreciated by the village.

With support from Brayton church and the wider circuit, and hard work from the local members, the church has grown and there are now regularly 20 at worship on a Thursday. The coffee morning provides a valuable community gathering place and the church is experimenting with café-style worship on a Sunday.[7]

It seems significant that, once Eggborough became a class, some people felt able to become members. Perhaps this was because there was now no expectation that they would have to take on roles of responsibility within the church but could rather use the gifts they had been given in the mission of the church. This is a good example of churches and a circuit cooperating in order to further mission in a particular village.

An incarnational approach

Building relationships is at the heart of working with others. This requires significant time, energy and patience. Leadership in rural multi-church groups is corporate, not individual, reflecting the complex multilevel and multipersonal decision making that is required. Rural leadership is also relational: the minister or lay leader is relating to human beings, not managing systems. These relationships between ministers and congregations need to be encouraging, supporting and enthusing, treating others as equals and remaining open to new ideas and approaches; and this must work in both directions.

A rural minister in the North Yorkshire Dales describes

her approach to being incarnational and missional in a large multi-church group and starting where people are in their faith.

I have looked for ways to be visible and available to those in the community who may not come to church. I will stop to chat at the school or farm gate if I am 'just passing'. Spending time around shops or the village centre can be fruitful. Several days a week, I will go to 'post a letter' and spend an hour or two in the village, doing a circuit of the village, talking to people I meet, hearing about what is going on (and no, I don't have a dog!). I find the places where people gather and spend time. For me it is at the little shop in one village, the lunch club in another, the local museum in another, and the lounge at the sheltered flats. The reason for all these things is that the heart of ministry is relationships. Building relationships and building trust takes time and there are no short cuts. I can tell the difference after five years in rural ministry. I am no longer new; I am now known and trusted.

Part of our ministry may be to change the local church culture. This must be done slowly but surely, in small steps, so that nothing is too scary. To work in this way you need to develop missionary eyes and ears and a missionary mind. I often pray that I will have eyes to see and ears to hear where God is at work, so that I am aware of his leading.

If you were planning to go abroad as a missionary, you would probably do some basic preparation and try to learn something of the language, customs and traditions of the place where you were going to live and work. You would want to have an idea of how to build relationships and how relationships work in that culture. You would also have to avoid making assumptions and imposing your own cultural expectations and views. This has been my approach to working in a rural multi-church group, where each congregation has a different history, experience and understanding, and where there are locals, incomers and visitors, all with different expectations of the church and the minister and different experiences of Christian faith.

I have worked intentionally to become part of the place and the culture. I have learned that it is important to recognise the differences between the farming community and the newer residents, and to learn to move in both cultures. For me, this is about being incarnational.

Leadership

'The role of the priest is to support the ministry of the church, not to do it.'[8] Increasingly, in the denominations in the countryside, mission, ministry and leadership will be a shared endeavour. These things will be shared by lay and ordained, and with more than one denomination. As rural churches evolve towards this reality, leadership for mission and ministry, by both ordained and lay, will require approaches that are different from those still frequently used today.

Most often, the position of leader is taken by an ordained priest, whether full-time, part-time or volunteer. Increasingly, lay people have significant leadership roles, either during a vacancy or due to the organisational structure of that group of churches. Realistically, a broad range of leadership styles is used, presenting a spectrum of approaches, usually depending on the situation and people involved. These styles include strategic or visionary, acting as a catalyst, seeking to involve others, enabling and encouraging, and oversight.

Some congregations will be eager to get involved in mission and ministry, develop their gifts and learn new skills; others will be more reticent. A spectrum of responses can be described:

- An understanding that ministers and lay leaders are there to provide professional services for the people, such as leading worship, visiting and so on.

- Tasks being delegated by the minister to others, who are allowed to help out.
- All baptised Christians sharing in ministry, with a move away from a hierarchical structure.

The transition to a collaborative approach to leadership, involving lay and ordained together, requires qualities and skills to be held across a number of people rather than all within the single person of the minister. Leaders are still needed but they need to be mindful of team dynamics and operate differently compared with a more traditional model. They need to balance the three functions of a leader:

- Getting the job done—achieving the task.
- Creating and developing a cohesive group—building and maintaining a team.
- Developing the individual—paying attention to physical, psychological, social, emotional and spiritual needs.[9]

In developing the ministry of lay people, we need to work with the skills and gifts we have, and encourage and develop them further. This may involve formal training, but, for many people, that may be inappropriate or ineffective; a less formal approach, perhaps even 'stealth training', may be more effective. Challenged on how to develop lay leadership in small, elderly, rural congregations, a senior bishop said that when faced with this situation as a parish priest, he told the congregation he could only be present once a month, but asked them to continue to meet weekly and read a simple liturgy. Some weeks later, hearing it was going well, he suggested they now add intercessions. In simple stages he enabled a traditional congregation to run most of their own services.

Some churches find the concept of 'the square' helpful, taken from an approach known as Lifeshapes.[10] This reflects Jesus' development of the twelve disciples—frankly, rather a motley crew, who in due course changed the world. It points to the amount of time Jesus spent with the disciples (rather than in front of the crowd), eating and sharing his life with them. The four sides of the square represent stages of development:

- **I do, you watch:** initially, Jesus adopted a directive leadership style, saying, 'Come and follow me' to the disciples, bringing the good news of the kingdom of God to towns and villages, and performing miracles.
- **I do, you help:** Jesus moved to a more coaching style, involving the disciples; for example, Mark 9:28–29 shows that they were doing miracles (and sometimes failing).
- **You do, I help:** this is a consensus approach; Jesus calls the disciples 'friends' (John 15:12–17) and sends out the Twelve with a clear briefing (Matthew 10).
- **You do, I watch:** after the disciples have been envisioned, enabled and equipped, they are empowered to start on the great commission (Matthew 28:18–20).

The point here is that church leaders cannot just tell people what to do and expect them to be able to pick it up. It is a process requiring considerable time and attention. It also requires humility. Any personal desire for glory must be tamed to encourage others.

In reflecting on the approach to leadership in which ministry and mission are shared, Robert Warren identified five key movements away from traditional practice.

- Being a conductor rather than a director—building on the gifts within the church rather than on those of the minister.
- Becoming a facilitator rather than a provider—enabling people to do for themselves rather than adopting a client mode.
- Being a permission giver rather than a permission withholder—allowing laity to shape and initiate.
- Steering rather than rowing—causing everything to be done as opposed to doing everything.
- Being a person rather than a parson—reflecting the incarnate Christ and being open and vulnerable as a part of this.[11]

These changes may be challenging for some and may lead to significant resistance. In some places there has to be an enormous paradigm shift in the approach and understanding of both congregations and clergy, and conflict will result. Where congregations are willing to take part in the tasks of mission and ministry, developing their own gifts and skills, there is great potential to develop and extend the kingdom of God.

A ministry of oversight?

Reflecting on his own experience of developing the ministry of lay people in rural multichurch groups, the Rt Revd Mark Rylands writes:

In the Church of England, we are moving into a period where there will be fewer stipendiary 'overseer' ministers and more non-stipendiary assistant and local lay ministers. It seems that rural ministry has been pioneering patterns of sustainable leadership for the whole church. We are already walking this path.

Rural ministers have been learning to be effective leaders in a different way in order to thrive. It is here that an understanding of leadership as 'episcope' can inspire and inform. A leadership of oversight, akin to the conductor of an orchestra, puts the emphasis on discerning the vocation and developing the talents of others rather than keeping ministry to the few or even the one. It encourages, enables and empowers others to use their gifts in God's service and hence discover their life in Christ. In this manner, a focus on waking up the dormant members of the body of Christ will lead to a more vibrant Christian witness making a difference in the wider community.

In this respect, my understanding of God as the Missioner has led me to see that the effective role of a vicar is more talent spotter than performer and more trellis builder than planter. In horticultural terms, God achieves the growth but he encourages us to help with the gardening. I was beginning to see that cultivating the ground and creating the right environment for plants to thrive would lead to sustainable growth.[12]

A shared understanding of participation and involvement, as well as the use of distributive leadership, is the starting point. The first step is to help people develop a sense of belonging and ownership of the concept. Use of tools such as a Mission Action Plan or a mission or community audit are helpful in taking these first steps. Where congregations are less willing to take part in the tasks of mission and ministry, it is a harder path to tread. Gently asking and encouraging can pay dividends but takes time and patience.

Practical experience of developing a ministry of oversight suggests that there are some key emphases that can assist with drawing people in and facilitating change.

- **Trust people.** Identify gifts and skills in others; facilitate their training, formation and authorisation (as necessary); provide back-up and guidance, then trust individuals and groups to work responsibly. With few exceptions, perfection is less important than the growth in experience and confidence. Good fruit, which perhaps is unexpected, may be among the results.
- **Prioritise interventions.** The function of oversight sometimes means offering guidance or conveying expectations but seldom 'stepping in' directly. Reserve 'intervention capital' for when it really matters, especially when boundaries or requirements need to be clarified.
- **Prioritise time.** Being intentional, honest and self-critical about use of time is essential, with priority needed for tasks that involve support, training and supervision. This has to be balanced carefully with tasks that can only be done by the minister. Adequate time for self and family is a top priority in the stewardship of time. Time management is the key area in which ministers' own expectations and those of others can draw ministers away from oversight towards unexamined, reactive immersion.
- **Core vocation.** Oversight should be exercised in conjunction with, and through, the ministries of word, sacrament and pastoral care. The minister remains an effective practitioner, fulfilling the original calling to ministry, not becoming solely a facilitator of others.
- **Enable communication.** In a complex multi-church environment, a minister can be either the chief enabler of communication throughout the system, modelling good practice, or a major barrier to it, especially if the minister concerned is a poor communicator. Email is a tool but should not replace personal communication; the harder

something is to say, the more likely it is that it needs to be said face to face. It is also necessary to communicate in as many different ways as possible, including email, websites and social media, as well as face to face, in pew sheets and village magazines and by putting posters on noticeboards.

- **Knowing and being known.** Exercising oversight wisely requires an incarnational approach: ministers know their people and are known by them. Living in only one of the settlements presents the challenge of being seen regularly in the other communities, which is not easy to achieve, especially where there are no obvious meeting places for those communities.

- **Importance of prayer.** Whatever a minister's tradition, the temptation to let daily prayer and biblical reflection slip down the list of priorities should be resisted. Sharing this activity with others can help in more ways than one. In the biggest picture of all, this is where the answer can be found to the fundamental ministerial question, 'What am I meant to be doing here?'[13]

It is important to emphasise that the skills needed in leadership of a large multi-church group cannot be found in a single person, ordained or lay. Leadership is multiple (Ephesians 4:11–12); alone we are incomplete.

> *It's time to end the myth of the complete leader; the flawless person at the top who's got it all figured out. In fact the sooner leaders stop trying to be all things to all people, the better off their organisations will be... Only when leaders come to see themselves as incomplete—as having both strengths and weaknesses—will they be able to make up for their missing skills by relating to others.*[14]

The diversity of skills and styles of leadership required is challenging and adds complexity to leadership within multi-church situations. This complexity reinforces the importance of shared leadership, both lay and ordained, to facilitate the development and growth of each church and community.

Creating space for mission

The ministry of administration

Many of the day-to-day tasks of administration can fall largely on clergy or a few individuals, and, particularly where there are several open churchyards within the group, this can be time-consuming and complex. An administrator can make a major positive difference to the effectiveness of teams, ministers and other voluntary roles. This is particularly valuable for forward planning, arranging events and regular activities, as well as supporting the provision of worship and the occasional offices.

A good administrator with enough time can significantly improve communications, prepare agendas and take minutes of meetings. Others work for only a few hours each week, and not all administrators are paid. However, any large voluntary structure, such as a multi-church group, needs an administrator or other responsible person to carry out this sort of work, lifting the burden from lay and ordained alike and creating time and space for other activities.

A learning community

In the Diocese of Bath and Wells, clergy leading multi-church groups can benefit from a regular gathering known as the '5+ Rural Learning Network'.[15] These gatherings offer time to explore current problems and are shaped to enable members to reflect and share experiences, providing some basis on which to develop further in the multi-church group context.

The former convenor and facilitator Steve Annandale admits that he saw members leaving a session with as many questions as when they arrived. But Steve feels that the value of the group is that others recognise the questions:

> Some have been able to reframe questions so they have become manageable—even solvable. This is a group that does not set out to deliver solutions but it does offer clarification and insight only feasible through shared experience. What is shared has the ring of credibility and the hope of being transformed into something that can be applied in deeply rural Somerset.

Membership of the 5+ group also helps to reduce isolation (particularly where clergy are working mostly by themselves), provides mutual support and offers a shared approach to developing new ideas and problem-solving.

Developing vision and cohesion

A large united parish in Yorkshire, with four churches, used a parish vision process to help the churches move forward and grow in faith together. Six areas were identified for further development.

The vicar comments:

> The process is on every PCC agenda, and each meeting includes a review of progress and future planning. We decided not to set a timetable, but to focus on one area at a time and 'work it' until we got to a good point to move on. In practice, we have worked for about a year on each area.

The six areas identified were prayer, learning more about the Bible, discipleship, worship, welcome and mission. Work on these areas has become incorporated into the life of the churches, helping to create a cohesive group of four churches and communities. It has greatly increased the involvement and ownership of lay people in the ministry and mission of their churches; it has also enabled the vicar to facilitate others and has created new opportunities for community engagement and mission.

To explore more about resourcing and training for multi-church ministry, see www.germinate.net/go/mcm.

Notes

1 Anthony Russell, *The Country Parson* (SPCK, 1993), p. 3
2 For more information, see *Released for Mission: Growing the rural church* (Archbishops' Council, 2015), pp.10–11: www.churchofengland.org/media/2148423/gs%20misc%20 1092%20-%20rural%20multi%20parish%20benefices.pdf
3 For example, *From Anecdote to Evidence* (Archbishops' Council, 2014). www.churchgrowthresearch.org.uk/report
4 W.J. Carter, *Team Spirituality* (Abingdon Press, 1997), p. 17
5 Quoted in J.A.T. Robinson, *The New Reformation* (SCM, 1965), p. 55
6 Constitution Practice and Discipline of the Methodist Church, CPD S/O 500. www.methodist.org.uk/ministers-and-office-holders/cpd
7 www.germinate.net/go/eggborough
8 Quoted from private communication to Jill Hopkinson by an Anglican priest responsible for a group of five churches
9 John Adair, quoted in Sally Nash, Jo Pimlott and Paul Nash, *Skills for Collaborative Ministry* (SPCK, 2008), p. 14
10 Mike Breen and Walt Kallestad, *A Passionate Life* (Kingsway, 2005)

11 Robert Warren, *A Time for Sharing: Collaborative ministry in mission* (Board of Mission of the Church of England, 1995)

12 Based on 'Multi-church ministry: pioneering leadership for today' in *Country Way* 55 (2010), p. 20: http://content.yudu.com/Library/A1rnt7/CountryWayIssue55/resources/index.htm

13 Based on personal communication of Simon Martin with Revd Preb Douglas Dettmer and Revd Canon Anna Norman-Walker, both of Exeter Diocese. See also Douglas Dettmer, 'What am I supposed to be doing here?' in *Country Way* 48 (2008). http://content.yudu.com/Library/A1rog7/CountryWayIssue48/resources/20.htm

14 Deborah Ancona, Thomas W. Malone, Wanda J. Orlikowski and Peter M. Senge, *In Praise of the Incomplete Leader* (Harvard Business Review, 2007). https://hbr.org/2007/02/in-praise-of-the-incomplete-leader/ar/1

15 See more on the 5+ Rural Learning Network, including details of how the sessions work, at www.germinate.net/go/fiveplusnetwork

Discipleship, nurture and training

Simon Martin

Making disciples was the activity into which Jesus put most of his ministry time. It was the challenge he set his disciples as his final command on earth. If we want to quantify and monitor our success as a church, then what counts is not the number of attendees but the number of people growing as disciples.

The Jesus model of discipleship is multifaceted. Key aspects include:

- Community: a small group eating, learning and engaged in ministry together
- The 'Lifeshapes' apprentice approach: Jesus built confidence, competence, experience and enthusiasm through what could be seen as the four sides of a square (see page 54):
  - I do, you watch: directive (Mark 1:15–18).
  - I do, you help: coaching (Mark 9:28–29).
  - You do, I help: consensus (John 15:12–17).
  - You do, I watch: delegation (Matthew 28:18–20).
- The involvement of invitation and challenge, fun and purpose.

Different approaches need to be taken, to adapt this model to different modern rural settings according to the context and resources available. Nevertheless, discipleship is likely to be in a small group, where lives are shared and there is challenge and purpose alongside invitation and fun. It is a lifelong process, ideally in an environment where learning and development of faith are natural for everyone.

A wide range of approaches and resources are available, some of which are helpful for small, rural congregations. In this chapter we reflect on Christian discipleship in rural contexts and explore some of the different approaches that have been used.

Discipleship and rural ministry

In 2011 the ARC published a research report on the training and resources available to rural churches: *Resourcing and Training for the Rural Church: Surveying the experience of contemporary practitioners and churchgoers*. Discipleship was one of the areas included in the study as it was felt to be important to understand whether rural contexts had a distinctive effect on how the content and approach of different resources could be used. In relation to nurture and discipleship, three key elements emerged: the content of the resources, the context in which they were used and the approach to the provision of training courses and encouragement of learning.

- There were often tensions between the content of resources for discipleship and nurture and the context in which they were being used. Resources from one tradition or another, or that were perceived to be very individualist, were often felt to be inappropriate.
- Materials produced for a general audience were often felt to be quite divorced from the circumstances of many rural churches, particularly in smaller and more isolated communities. In rural contexts, the assumption that there

is a large number of people in a group or congregation, or the use of urban descriptive terms such as 'neighbourhood', can contribute to disengagement from the material by participants.

- The approach of many training providers is to centralise provision of training, which fails to take into consideration distance and accessibility, travel times or locally available support.

Alongside these three key elements, our research and the findings of others suggested that a lack of discipleship resources was not a major problem. Other factors were also important, such as lack of understanding of the resources available, an absence of a culture of learning or a poor understanding of what discipleship is.

'There is no need for extra resources. Rather more helpful would be a reference point for what there is.' As this comment from a minister indicates, far from there being too few to choose from, many people found that there were too many resources and were unable to decide which was most suitable for their situation. Signposting, evaluation and recommendation were needed most.

Many rural church leaders recognised that their churches had no real culture of nurture. As one rural vicar revealed, 'In a lot of these communities, we're very strong on... community focus; we're probably not so strong on discipleship.' Another indicated 'surprise at the lack of interest in or tradition of any teaching, study or discipleship in the group'. The need in these circumstances was for assistance in how to encourage and develop a learning culture.

For some, the underlying concern was that even regular churchgoers were unsure of what discipleship involved.

One rural lay leader illustrated this: 'Being a member of the Sunday congregation doesn't guarantee faith development. Being part of a small group doesn't guarantee it either.' For others, there was concern that introducing new initiatives was unhelpful in small, rural church contexts. This was not because of specific opposition to new things, but because of the potential to overwhelm small, often elderly and under-resourced congregations.

What resources are being used?

The research identified the pros and cons of different resources and training courses for supporting and developing nurture and discipleship.

Most frequently, courses such as Alpha or Emmaus or denominational courses were used. In many cases, though, dissatisfaction was expressed with such material, as it was felt to be unsuited to the needs of people from small, rural congregations. There was also concern expressed about the often-unspoken assumption that churches would have a large congregation and well-resourced clergy staff team, and about a perceived suburban bias and middle-class approach. These courses also usually required a large number of people to deliver them effectively. Some general resources were not felt to be contextual, specific or practical enough; they also had less to do with learning to live out a Christian life in the rural context, and more to do with being conformed to a predetermined pattern or absorbing largely theoretical knowledge. In particular, they allowed little room for users or participants to raise and handle their own issues.

A small but significant proportion of respondents also noted that many of the general materials had a focus on discipleship that was geared to individual growth and development, to the detriment of learning and being nurtured communally as part of the body of Christ.

The research project found that locally produced discipleship materials were widely used and valued. Nurture courses that were most effective in helping people to grow in faith were those produced locally and in response to the issues raised by participants. These materials might start with an initial open session, in which enquirers were invited to set the agenda for the questions that they wished to be explored over the lifetime of the group (typically six to eight weeks). This had the great advantage of genuinely seeking to begin with the questions people had, rather than the questions that we wished they had in order to fit our prearranged exposition of the gospel.

However, some caution is needed, as this approach is demanding and time-consuming, and wise leadership requires the ability to be flexible and responsive while still leading participants on a journey of encounter and discovery that has Christ and the gospel at its heart. It contrasts with and complements the more fixed model for nurture courses, which can be more appropriate for deepening the discipleship of those who have already made a commitment to following Christ.

Frequently, good-quality general resources are 'rural proofed' or adapted in-house to meet local needs. This, too, requires measures of time, gifts and experience that may not be widely available.

The rest of this chapter describes approaches and resources that will help rural churches and training providers to choose or develop resources appropriate for their specific circumstances and needs. There are four overlapping strands.

- Case studies reflecting good practice in relation to approach, context or content of resources.
- Suggestions for 'rural proofing' general materials so that they can more closely fit the needs of small rural churches and communities.
- Identifying and evaluating good resources.
- Reflecting on how the best approaches to Christian growth and nurture are often provided locally.

Approaches to discipleship

Discipleship, nurture and faith development are essentially communal processes. Christian faith and walking in the footsteps of Christ take place in two contexts that are communal: the local church as the body of Christ, and the communities in which the follower of Christ lives on a daily basis (which certainly include both the workplace and the home). Learning and practice are most effective when done in community. In most cases this is best done in small groups, although, for some rural churches, the whole regular congregation may be the equivalent of a small group.

The practice of ministry is an essential part of discipleship. From the calling of Jesus' very first disciples, an apprentice-type model of growth and development in following Christ has always been at the heart of the most effective methods. We learn best and most retentively by putting our learning into practice. Again, this is often best encouraged in a small group environment that overlaps with, and feeds into, the wider church and the community the church serves.

Cell church

Cell church—a number of small groups known as cells, which meet regularly and form the core of a church community—

can be considered a good approach to discipleship, especially in rural communities. Revd Sally Gaze describes her own experience of continuing the process of discipleship for those who had attended Alpha, and of gently coaxing more mature Christians into lay leadership through cell churches in rural communities. She makes the following key points about this as a contemporary approach to discipleship in rural contexts.[1]

A cell church approach:

- delivers the small church from having to be all things to all people.
- widens choice about how to 'be church'.
- challenges an 'attendance mentality'.
- helps to create and sustain Christian community, which is crucial to effective faith development.
- is a natural lead-in from evangelism, helping to nurture and develop new Christians in the same participative style in which they found faith.
- fits with the best of rural church—local, lay-led and small.
- helps to release the gifts of lay people.
- depends on and encourages networking and personal relationships (which is normal in most rural communities).

'Steps': pattern, presence and pilgrimage[2]

Revd Eddie Green tells how a group of rural parishes in north Oxfordshire developed an approach to corporate nurture that is sacramental and reflective, meeting their particular needs.

Steps is hard to define—it isn't a home group and it isn't a discussion group. In a sense, *Steps* is *Steps*, Christians supporting each other in the Way.

In the past, small groups, even seasonal study groups, have struggled.

Typically people managed three or four sessions out of a six-week course. *Steps* grew out of this context: it involves a group of people, lay and ordained, meeting together once a month as they are able, and committed to a simple rhythm or rule of life. The structure of the gatherings is less important than the atmosphere, but refreshments are always enjoyed, and Compline is always said in the nearest parish church. A core group of people come every month; others drop in as they are able. The commitment to the community is not so much about meetings, but about the threefold rhythm or rule that we explore together.

- **Pattern:** *Steps* offers a simple shape of prayer based on the midday office and Compline, a pattern seen in a wider context too as we celebrate the saints and seasons. When we meet, this pattern shapes our meeting. We do not meet to discuss finances or hot-topic theology, but to be open and honest about our spirituality, something Anglicans frequently feel they need permission to do. When we meet, there is input of many sorts, besides prayer.
- **Presence:** Group members learn together what it means to be visible Christians in our communities and our social networks, which *Steps* recognises as a shared responsibility. A growing confidence is found in being open about our faith with each other, which spills over into the way we interact with people in our communities.
- **Pilgrimage:** Some members have been Christians for a long time, while others are newer or returners to faith. Recently, barriers have crumbled as we realised that our weaknesses enabled us in our shared priestly ministry: wherever we think we are in spiritual terms, there is something we can offer. Our pilgrimage together is essentially spiritual, but physical journeys can be part of it, especially as we travel around the benefice.

The threefold rule we adopted was not an accident; it was a response to the particular challenges of being a rural Christian in north Oxfordshire. Others considering a similar community would need to reflect on their context and a suitable rule, although I suspect there is considerable overlap.

Multiple, grouped churches

Some approaches to nurture and discipleship are particularly useful for rural churches and churchgoers, not so much because of the content of the material but more because of the means of delivery. Examples from two dioceses in the Church of England, each with large numbers of rural churches, illustrate this, where the deanery is being used to deliver training and courses.

Revd Canon Clare Sanders, from the Diocese of Edmundsbury and Ipswich, describes one such development.

> Many rural churches are small and may be quite isolated from other rural congregations. On their own, they often have real difficulty in resourcing and running high-quality training for lay people. Some of the best solutions to this problem require compromise: sacrificing some of the benefits of running a programme as locally as possible, while not offering such a course so centrally that it becomes difficult for local church members to travel and attend.

Woodbridge Deanery[3] provides a case study in how to achieve such a compromise and still provide an appropriate, practical discipleship programme that none of the individual parishes alone could offer. Clare describes their underlying purpose: 'There wasn't... much happening for people which linked their learning into their practice of faith, whether in acknowledged ministerial positions, such as Reader or lay evangelist, or simply as adult Christians.' A termly programme of meetings and events is used to focus on a different topic, such as worship, pastoral ministry, biblical study or understanding church buildings.

Clare continues:

There was opportunity to learn and be stretched, to apply that learning to our local church. There was encouragement to go back and tell the PCC about what had been learnt. Just as importantly, people began to talk to one another and discover what was happening in other places. People felt encouraged and less isolated, and they appreciated that they weren't alone in being part of a small but faithful church community, as they were part of something bigger. The concept of deanery began to have a human face—indeed, 30 to 40 faces of people who weren't necessarily the Deanery Synod representatives, but were lovingly serving in their village churches and communities. The great joy was that when it came to the final session, there was a request for a party, and offers of wine and refreshments.

Ross and Archenfield Deanery is in the Diocese of Hereford. The deanery started an annual eight-week course called *Growin' Faith*,[4] which aimed to nurture the discipleship of congregation members, develop individual parish mission and ministry, and reinforce a coherent vision for the life of the church across a large rural area. This course has been delivered every autumn since 2010, while in 2013 a shorter spring course was introduced as well, in response to demand and the very positive results from the previous three years' programmes.

Revd Elaine Goddard, Rural Dean, reflects on the impact of *Growin' Faith*.

The course has informed and strengthened the members of the ministry team, which has in turn underpinned the strategic work of the church in my own benefice. An Ordained Local Minister in training has also used the courses as part… of her training. There is evidence that capturing the imagination of people through their attendance at the course has made a contribution to church growth in the deanery. Though not intentionally an evangelistic programme, the courses have seen people bringing others along to share in the sessions. This has been an added but unexpected outcome in a deanery where an overt approach to evangelism doesn't seem to be effective.

The United Reformed Church (URC) has employed a similar approach to benefit some of their small and rural churches. Resources have been produced annually within the Eastern Synod (the most rural in the URC) that focus on some of the key needs of the churches. They are designed to nurture congregation members, to support practical involvement in the mission and ministry of the local churches, and to be used by groups of churches together. The element of support between churches in this way has been of real value. One course participant commented, 'It's good to know that we are not alone.'

Revd Peter Ball, Mission and Training Officer for the URC Eastern Synod, explains the approach used.

After initial consultation with our 147 churches, it was clear that what they wanted were resources that could be used at a local church level to aid pastoral care, outreach and mission to local communities. I add one booklet a year, with the topics coming from suggestions made to me by local church members. All the materials are freely available from our Synod website.[5] They have proved to be a popular resource and, in several instances, a group of local churches have come together to study the resource and learn from each other's experiences.

These discipleship and training resources include courses on pastoral care, ageing and spirituality, conflict resolution, worship, mission and belonging.[6]

This type of approach, bringing together people from

several different churches, is relevant for multi-church groups, circuits, deaneries or synod areas where a critical mass for both attendance and delivery would be difficult to attain for a single church or a small group of churches. Material such as *Steps* and *Sustaining Faith in the Future* (see page 75) were created for rural multi-church situations, and *Your SHAPE for God's Service* (see page 76) has been used extensively in these situations.

'Ready, Steady, Grow'[7]

This started life as an ecumenical Lent course in rural Gloucestershire, based largely on two workbooks for the rural church: *Seeds in Holy Ground* from the Church of England, which takes a practical approach to issues facing rural churches, and *Presence* from the Methodist Church, which looks at the wider issues of being church in today's countryside.

Ready, Steady, Grow has adapted material from both workbooks to provide a tool for growth and discipleship in small congregations and groups of rural churches. It is intended for use by churchgoers who want to understand more about the ministry and mission of their churches and their own role within them. Running through it is a focus on learning about the local communities and the churches' engagement with them.

In each session there are resources for activity, information gathering, discussion, Bible study, worship and prayer, linked to a series of practical opportunities to develop what has been learnt. Key to each session is the opportunity for discussion around a topic relevant to the particular churches and communities represented. Participants are able to reflect on their own contexts and issues within a clear framework.

The five themes are:

- Getting ready
- The priestly church
- The prophetic church
- The evangelising church
- Ready to grow

Where the overall course leads will depend on where the group starts from, and the first session determines that starting point, while the final week looks back at the journey and plans what will happen next. *Ready, Steady, Grow* is a resource that is intended as a springboard for further faith development and active discipleship.

'Sustaining Faith in the Future'[8]

Sustaining Faith in the Future was initially developed as a Lent course for several small churches in rural Worcestershire. It was designed to help congregations to identify key issues corporately and create a space and time for the challenges to be addressed.

The course focuses on some of the most pressing needs of rural congregations, providing opportunity for small groups to reflect, pray, study scripture, look at simple case studies, and discuss and consider practical outcomes for each congregation as a whole. Six themes are explored:

- Buildings: blessing or burden?
- Administration: round pegs and square holes
- Worship: make a joyful noise to the Lord
- Working together: sing, choirs of angels
- Vocation: a pilgrim people
- Evangelism: the dreaded 'E' word

Every session includes a discussion about what the churches should be doing, and it is suggested that the answers are recorded. This provides food for reflection by PCCs and small congregational groups on what might be done practically and how decisions could be implemented. On this basis, the sessions need to include members of decision-making bodies such as church councils, and should be seen as just one part of ongoing faith development and discipleship.

'Your SHAPE for God's Service'[9]

This tool is designed to help lay people discern gifts, skills and vocations for service in God's name. It emphasises confidence-building, faith development and whole-life discipleship. It enables people to find out the shape that God has made them and to use that understanding to serve God in the church, the community and the workplace. It is appropriate for all kinds of churches, especially small ones whose members are not confident about having anything to offer. The key elements it covers are spiritual gifts, motivation, abilities and skills, personality and experiences.

Revd Canon Amiel Osmaston, Ministry Development Officer from the Diocese of Carlisle and author of the course, reveals something of its ethos, use and approach.

Originating in 2006, *Your SHAPE* has been deliberately made available cheaply and simply, so anyone can adapt it to suit their context. To my surprise, the materials have spread widely, with well over 500 groups having used them, including numerous rural churches in a wide range of settings; and it has proved applicable well beyond the boundaries of the Anglican Church.

But however good the course is, we can't grow disciples just by doing courses. We must create opportunities for people to use their gifts. Many churches ask people to volunteer time and talents, making lists of gifts and abilities, but then do little in the way of follow-up, which is very frustrating for people, leaving them feeling undervalued and rejected. So an essential part of *Your SHAPE* is the practical support and encouragement given to participants during the course itself and afterwards, to help discern ways of using their gifts. This only works if the minister is open to sharing ministry and is not threatened by others' gifts. One rural parishioner wrote wryly, 'Some people found the *SHAPE* course very helpful, but, having discovered their gift, they weren't able to exercise it within the church—or not to date! If the vicar is not prepared to allow people to exercise their gifts, it rather blunts the effects.'

One training adviser suggests, 'Discipleship is more about being than doing. Many similar courses focus on the gifts rather than the person, and it is vital to see 'people as people, not simply as doers of jobs in the church'. *Your SHAPE* does this admirably.' A rural church leader who has used the course several times indicates, 'It is not about simply getting people to recognise their gifts. Rather, it is about helping nurture their Christian walk in the context of the local church. There is nothing individualistic about *Your SHAPE*— the growth of the participants together is an essential part of developing the whole church.'

Other resources

There is particular value in small, isolated churches sending a group to a big event such as New Wine or Spring Harvest. These events tend to be urban- or suburban-focused; how-ever, the high standard of teaching and seminars, the inspi-ration of seeing so many people worshipping God and the power of the Holy Spirit at work, and the opportunity to spend time with fellow church members, can be an invaluable boost on the discipleship journey.

There is also, of course, a vast range of resources available for individual and group study, online and in print. These range from specific group discipleship resources, such as *Life on the Frontline* by The London Institute for Contemporary Christianity,[10] to daily Bible reading notes such as those from BRF[11] or Wordlive from Scripture Union,[12] to materials covering specific issues, themes or life stages.

Supporting nurture and discipleship

What support is available for rural congregations that have limited resources and few members?

Discipleship champions

This initiative brings together people who are passionate about growing disciples, with the aim of enabling them to enthuse the wider church and helping them to equip congregations and groups of churches for discipleship.

Revd Caroline Wickens has been responsible for developing discipleship in the West Midlands Methodist Districts and for resourcing local church discipleship through setting up a regional network of discipleship champions.

> One of my roles has been enabling people to explore God's call to them, encouraging them to consider new areas of service and discipleship and to support each other in small exploration groups. We have a responsibility to enable all Christians to explore God's purposes for them. One strapline has been, 'What does God want you to do with the next bit of your life?'
>
> It has become increasingly difficult to sustain a full programme for this. What could be done next? How could we sustain the benefits we had

gained? I decided to set up a discipleship network. Members come from the 25 circuits of the West Midlands. Some members are ministers, some are lay leaders; some come from the conurbation, others from the rural depths of Herefordshire or Shropshire. All share an enthusiasm for developing their own discipleship and, equally importantly, for helping others access resources to deepen theirs.

The network we have created has two major purposes:

• To allow members to support each other by sharing their interest and enthusiasm. A passion for discipleship, like any other passion, is easier to sustain among friends. Alongside this, members are invited to share good practice within their own circuits, swapping ideas and sharing learning from their own experiences.

• To receive information and training from those in the church who do have the opportunity to spend time developing resources for discipleship. The champions then act as both a conduit and a catalyst for this training to be used in churches and circuits.

The feedback I get from participants is that the difficulties involve getting the new insights taken up in their circuits. However, as the network's profile is growing across the area, circuit leaders are getting more accustomed to looking our way when they need resources for helping their congregations follow Jesus more closely.[13]

Resource networks

How do you resource small, dispersed rural congregations and their leaders, lay or ordained? This is a vital question for many providers of training or resources. There exists a very real tension between the fact that the best resourcing and training for lay people takes place locally, and the reality that many centralised or regional church structures find it hard to equip and supply facilitators or trainers at this level and so tend to operate much more centrally. There is a similar tension between realising that discipleship and nurture occur best when responding to and incorporating the local needs of those who are undertaking a journey of spiritual formation, and the time and expertise needed to produce flexible materials or adapt existing resources to do this.

Hereford Diocese is a good example of a very rural church constituency where these factors influence the way the congregations of rural churches can be nurtured and supported. Revd Caroline Pascoe, Lay Development Officer in the Diocese of Hereford, describes how the resource networks function.[14]

We have an amazing pool of talent and expertise in this diocese and a commitment to collaboration. We are growing diocesan resource networks to help us all access that shared talent and expertise and find out more easily about the great resources and support available right across the diocese, so that we can all learn and grow together. The network is being developed to research, create, recommend, publicise and offer an excellent range of resources to help people grow as disciples and live as disciples 24/7. Our work builds on and extends the wide range of learning opportunities that have been available locally and centrally in the diocese. We see the network's role as helping participants to think through what they need or the ideas they have, pointing them to useful resources, putting them in touch with a member of the network who is in their area or has the particular expertise they need, and sometimes offering local training.

The diocesan discipleship resource network currently provides:

- regular news updates
- ideas, advice and support on using the resources

- help with setting up, running or leading local discipleship courses and events
- training in skills to lead small groups
- a place to share local ideas, resources, expertise and stories
- coordinated training across several deaneries
- the development of a discipleship audit

Formal lay ministry training

The principles of an apprentice approach and nurture in community are illustrated by the Authorised Lay Ministry programme developed by Worcester Diocese. This does not have a specific rural brief, but more than half of its participants in the first two years were from rural parishes. Although the primary goal is the development of lay ministers with specific skills and knowledge, it also has a substantial element of nurture. This nurturing and enabling of people takes place within local congregations, which in turn helps the congregation to grow in faith, as well as helping to equip them for service in both local church and community. Six streams are currently offered: children's and youth work, community work, evangelism, parish administration, pastoral work, and leading worship. One current tutor says, 'For many on the [programme], it is as much about their own faith development as it is about equipping them for a specific ministry.'

The emphasis throughout is on practical elements of the Christian faith, on learning corporately, and on applying what has been learnt collaboratively through the local church. The first year is a single training programme, offered at various locations, to assist those in isolated places. Participants are then supported for a further four years as they develop their involvement in their local parishes and benefices. Growth and nurture are not restricted to the first year, but happen just as much in the subsequent years, encouraging the habit of discipleship for all who are involved.

One participant who followed the children's and youth work stream talks of her continuing faith journey in subsequent years as she works with children through her parish: 'I am on a parallel journey with the children, and my desire to grow spiritually has intensified... I know that my appetite to grow in faith will need further feeding.'

Another participant also highlights the nurture and formation element experienced in following the pastoral stream and serving through her local church: 'Reflection on the importance of being unfinished was thought-provoking. It emphasised that we are never quite finished, our lives constantly changing and being shaped by our communities, the Bible and God's Spirit. Importantly for me, this meant it was OK to make mistakes... as we learn from them.'[15]

As well as local approaches such as this example from Worcester Diocese, extension studies offered by many Bible colleges give an opportunity to apply learning to the local context and individual ministry, while various colleges, networks and organisations offer regionally based training.

'Rural proofing' nurture and discipleship

A resource for discipleship or nurture designed for general use would benefit from a consideration of how it might need to be adapted to fit the needs of small rural congregations in multi-church groups. 'Rural proofing' is as much about ensuring that the material is contextually appropriate as it is about responding to issues of small numbers or travel distance.

The following list offers some simple guidelines for thinking through the 'rural proofing' of nurture and discipleship resources.[16]

- Deliverable for small and potentially isolated and dispersed churches and communities?
- Offers varied approaches to learning and actively involves participants?
- Appropriate for small groups, offering an informal atmosphere?
- Encouraging group participants to share in the leadership of the programme?
- Easily adaptable, to provide opportunities for participants to bring their own concerns, situations and needs to the discussion?
- Resonating with local rural culture and community norms?
- Offers the opportunity to encourage biblical and ethical reflection on local issues and concerns?

Further resources

See www.germinate.net/go/discipleship for more material on discipleship and nurture in rural communities.

Notes

1 www.germinate.net/go/discipleshiptoday
2 www.germinate.net/go/steps
3 www.germinate.net/go/lawd
4 www.germinate.net/go/growinfaith
5 www.urc-eastern.org.uk/td-locall-church/focus-booklets
6 You can find more on the URC approach at www.germinate.net/go/urcsuffolk, including free access to all the course material
7 More detail on *Ready, Steady, Grow* and the full course can be found at www.germinate.net/go/rsg

8 More detail on *Sustaining Faith in the Future* and the full course can be found at www.germinate.net/go/sustainingfaith

9 More information, as well as the full *Your SHAPE* course as a free download, and other materials, are available at www.germinate.net/go/yourshape

10 www.licc.org.uk/imagine-church/resources/life-on-the-frontline

11 www.biblereadingnotes.org.uk

12 www.wordlive.org

13 www.germinate.net/go/disciplechampions

14 www.germinate.net/go/resourcenetwork

15 www.germinate.net/go/almdiscipleship

16 www.germinate.net/go/evaluatenurture

Worship

Caroline Hewlett

Christian worship in rural churches is still part of the fabric
of rural community life. It is something that the older local
people grew up with and in which some continue to take a
regular part. It can be ordinary and accessible, regular and
predictable. The round of worship continues week by week,
as it has done for centuries in some communities, whether or
not many people gather to share in the services.

God in the ordinary

Kathleen Norris describes how, in a monastic community,
'prayer rolls on, as daily as marriage and washing dishes'.[1]
This is a good description of worship in many small, rural
churches. There are regular worshippers, who make up the
visible body of Christ week by week, but there are also those
in the local community who rarely participate in services
and yet have a strong sense of belonging to 'our church'.
Daily prayer, weekly Holy Communion, harvest festivals
and Christmas and Easter celebrations come round and are
marked in the particular way of worship of that community,
the church year running in parallel to the cycle of the year
on the land. Rural worship is, for the most part, ordinary,
yet particular because it is connected to its local context. At
its best it underpins the life of the local community, whose
members recognise its value and its part in the identity of
that place. The knowledge that worship continues regularly

on their behalf and in their community is usually enough for most people, although they may take a more active part when worship connects directly with their lives, through baptisms, weddings, funerals and festivals.

Paula Gooder writes, 'If "special" is what we aim for, then by extension "ordinary" is disappointing. The problem with this is that sometimes—often, in fact—the special is embedded deep within the ordinary but it takes a well-trained eye to notice it.'[2]

Worship in rural churches is rooted in the ordinary—and the ordinary, when rooted in the place of worship that belongs to generations of a community, becomes important and holy. Paula Gooder also reflects that 'the monastic life draws people deeply into ordinariness through the passing of time in a particular place and it is in that ordinariness that they encounter God'.[3] In the parish where I am currently the vicar, one of the questions we have asked ourselves when thinking about mission is 'What does it mean to be the people of God in this place and at this time?' In other words, we begin by recognising that our particular mission as the local church begins with the ordinary things of our life together here and now, in the wider context of all that has gone before.

Some ancient rural churches began as part of monastic foundations, and this sense of the round of worship in the ordinary seems to be in their DNA. Worship persists, marking out life in times and seasons and holding the life of the community in the life of God, however many people attend services. Numbers are not really the point of worship, and measuring them may not tell us very much. Of course, we count the numbers and submit them to our church organisations each year—how many come each week and each month, how many took Communion at Christmas or Easter—but in the gathering of those who are present to worship, what matters are the ordinary and the individual. Joan is there because her husband died last year and she is feeling her way back to faith. Bill has been churchwarden for many years and is rooted in the place, like the hefted sheep on the hills outside the windows.[4] Mary has married into a new community and is looking for friends and a place to belong and be known.

Rural life operates on its own small scale, and small numbers in worship services should not be seen as a problem but as an opportunity for knowing and being known in a way that is not possible in a bigger congregation. Reading back through the service registers can give us a clue to this: the numbers and pattern of attendance may not have changed much for many years, although in a small congregation there can be a sense of lack or failure. These congregations of faithful people can be reassured that they are part of a chain of worship going back through the generations in that place. They are symbols now of the way that God has been, and still is, at work in their community.

Adapting to change

The ordinary round of worship, cycling through the church year, can give the impression that nothing ever changes. However, huge change has happened in rural life over the years, and there is a sense now that things are changing more quickly than ever before. Worship has changed too, adapting to the changes in life and attitudes, seeking to be more accessible and finding ways to connect with and speak into the lives of those whom the local church serves. Patterns of worship services have changed as there are fewer ministers to serve the same number of church communities. Rural churches may now have services once or twice a month, instead of twice each Sunday with Sunday school in between, as those with long memories still describe.

Sunday schools may no longer take place in rural areas, but rural churches are able to have close links with their village schools, especially if they are church controlled or aided primary schools, when the minister and others have genuine opportunities to worship with the children. Where there are no children or young people in the church services on Sundays, church members can be encouraged to take part in the life of their local primary school, as governors or volunteer helpers, as a way of connecting with and being a Christian influence in the lives of the young people in their community. Children and their parents can be invited to church for worship at Christmas and Easter, or the school may be willing to prepare an activity for a Mothering Sunday or Harvest Festival service. Significant moments, such as the school leavers' service at the end of the academic year, can be marked in church, with children and regular members of the church congregation taking part together. The vicar and church members may be able to participate in worship in the school in various forms, including daily collective worship, prayer times or other assemblies that take place.

Following the wind of the Spirit

In rural churches, there may be some resistance to change, but there is also the opportunity to see where the wind of the Spirit is blowing and to go with that wind of change. In my role as vicar of a rural parish with four churches, I have found that if I can discern what is 'in the air', which way the wind is blowing, and follow that lead, that is when change happens. New ideas and ways of doing things have their moment; this is God's timing, *kairos* timing, and we cannot push it or make it happen. Looking back afterwards, it is usually possible to see God at work in sometimes small changes that have made it possible for surprising new things to grow and to flourish.

Denise Owen, priest-in-training from an urban background who spent a month on placement in a deeply rural parish, observed that 'the PCC was open to the purchase of new hymn books—so they clearly aren't against change if they see the need'. In that parish, the purchase of new hymn books gave an opportunity to introduce some new hymns and music. This was done through regular open sessions called 'Come and sing', in which regular worshippers and local friends were invited to a relaxed time of singing, which included both well-known and new hymns. The sessions were led by organists and other musicians and allowed regular worshippers to enjoy coming together to sing and become familiar with some newer music before they met it in worship services. It also gave an opportunity to those who did not come to church regularly to enjoy a time of singing, and to make or improve connections and relationships with church people.

Working with the challenges of multi-parish ministry

The typical pattern of services in a multi-parish benefice or large circuit means that the vicar or minister may lead worship only once or twice a month in each church, and/or may have to leave to get to another church as soon as the service is over.

Being pastoral

Denise Owen, the priest-in-training quoted above, decided during her placement in a rural multi-parish benefice to observe how far it was possible to exercise a pastoral ministry in a context where the minister is not able to stay to engage with people for a lengthy period at the end of each Sunday service.

She reflected:

> Being pastoral is a difficult one in the context of the Sunday morning dash between churches. What I would say is that in the small scattered community in these two valleys, the priest is very visible, more than in an urban setting, and that opportunity for pastoral encounters happened all the time. I felt that the 'public' role of the 'local vicar' was important. For the people in the congregation, I think they understood the pressure of time and the need to move on to the next service. I think they also understood that if they wanted to speak to you, then you would make yourself available at another time.

This can be a challenge when new people arrive in church and the minister doesn't get an opportunity to connect with them at the end of the service. It means that the members of the congregation need to have an understanding of, and maybe some training in, welcome and pastoral care so that they are in a position to begin to draw visitors into the life of the church. The more the congregation can be helped to understand themselves as the body of Christ in that locality, the more effective this approach will be, and it will become a natural and integral part of their welcome and outreach.

Teaching and preaching

One of the other practical challenges for a minister in a multi-church arrangement is that of preaching and teaching the Bible in the context of worship. The reality of service patterns and the need for ministers to travel between services means that there may be only 10–15 minutes per fortnight in each church for this purpose. This, along with the limitations of the lectionary readings and a lack of familiarity with the Bible in some congregations, requires a variety of creative approaches.

Revd Canon Ann Chapman, a vicar in Wensleydale, North Yorkshire, has tried a more participative approach to teaching and preaching during more than ten years of ministry in that place. Ann was particularly struck by the work of Paulo Friere, a 20th-century Brazilian educator and philosopher. She describes how she learned that teaching adults could be about 'understanding people's experience, to use that to help them learn, and so that they learn they have something to bring'.

This led Ann into using 'conversation sermons' in a variety of forms. She commented wryly that these were never popular, but she remained committed to that style of teaching because 'until I know where that person is in their understanding of scripture, I am making assumptions about their understanding'.

She gave the congregation a sheet with the readings for each week printed out in full, so that everyone had the scriptures in front of them. Ann then asked, 'What does this reading say to you?' and led the congregation into a discussion to help them to engage with the texts. This was not a case of the vicar avoiding work—she always wrote a sermon as well—but she tried to be flexible and to use whatever was given to her by those who participated, in order to move the individuals in the congregation on in their understanding and journey of faith.

The response was mixed. She once overheard a comment from one person to another: 'Why do you have a vicar who asks you what you think?' The feedback from some members of the congregation was that 'it took too long', or they 'didn't like the inane comments made by others'. Others didn't want to feel that they might be pointed at or put on the spot, so Ann was careful not to do that. She persevered with the approach because she thought it was important for those who worshipped to fully engage with the scriptures and she recognised that this way of learning needed time to grow and develop.

Another approach to preaching for a short amount of time in a service is to use what has been described as a 'Marmite sermon'—a small amount and very concentrated. This is a spoken sermon, but with a focus on just one word, phrase, thought or major idea, which can then be explored in depth in the short time available.

Growing discipleship

Much of the work on growing disciples in a rural church needs to be done in the context of Sunday worship. In principle, small groups offer an opportunity for growing discipleship through more intimate worship, deeper personal relationships and shared outreach. However, in many rural areas, there is no culture of visiting others' homes, taking on leadership or sharing faith and feelings. In particular, programmes such as the Alpha course, which offer an opportunity to discuss personal faith in an anonymous group, are unlikely to be either anonymous or confidential in the countryside. Any person going to a group to talk about faith in a small community would know the others in the group, and may be related to them. Furthermore, the timescale of coming to faith over a few weeks, which is built into this type of course, is faster than life and thought in rural areas, where change may happen over years and decades. The image of a lifelong journey of discipleship, with stopping-off places to pause and reflect, may be more helpful than a programmed way of coming to faith. This is not a criticism of any particular course, but a note that the models used by such courses reflect a suburban rather than a rural culture.

Engaging with the familiar

It is worth taking time to encourage regular worshippers to look more closely at the forms of words that they use in worship. Most Anglican Communion services will use The Book of Common Prayer or Common Worship for their liturgy.

Denise Owen observes, 'In general terms, I'd say that a traditional Anglican Communion service is what people expected and most appreciated. I think this fed their sense of themselves as believers and people committed to the church.' Those who have grown up in church and have been regular worshippers for many years often know the liturgy so well that they can recite it by heart, and they may choose not to have a book in front of them during a service. The advantage of this is that the words are deep within people and they can draw on them for their own prayer life; the disadvantage is that the liturgy is so well known that it can be recited without engagement.

Soon after I arrived in my current churches, we bought some new Common Worship booklets, and we held some evening groups to explore the Common Worship service of Holy Communion. We went through the liturgy section by section, initially to help familiarise ourselves with the layout of the new book, but also to discuss the meaning and reason for each section. Those who had worshipped for many years commented that they found new depths and riches in the very familiar words and actions by looking at them in this way. This is one way of helping people who have been part of church for a long time to own and grow in their personal faith, starting from a familiar place. As their confidence grows, they can be encouraged and taught to speak about faith and to share it with others. This is the beginning of helping people to discover their own ministry in the local body of Christ.

Sharing in ministry: being the body of Christ

One of the roles of the minister is to encourage lay people into finding and exercising their ministry. This may be simply about providing training and resources and giving permission for an idea to grow; sometimes it will be a longer process, as those who come to church learn to understand themselves as members of the body of Christ, with gifts to offer, and then as ministers in that context.

In 2007, a group of regular worshippers at a small rural church in a tourist area realised that the pattern of services in their group of churches meant that they would not usually have a service at the time when Back to Church Sunday came round (usually the last Sunday in September). With encouragement from their minister, they planned and ran a service, and were pleased to welcome 15 locals and visitors.

One person from the congregation read the Bible, another led prayers, someone with musical ability chose hymns and played the organ, and others welcomed visitors and made the tea. One lady wrote and gave a short reflective talk, which was well received and was the start of her exploring a way into licensed ministry. The following year, the same group decided to lead four services, one each month through the summer. They also planned and led their own Palm Sunday service, including a procession and palm crosses. The members of this group are now able to plan and run services in their church and are encouraged by their minister to do it several times a year.

A group of six lay people in a rural church decided to start a prayer group. They met to read the Bible and they decided to work from a book that led them into an imaginative, Ignatian style of prayer. This was helpful and led them to contact and get to know an Anglican priest who spent time teaching them to pray and to lead others into the scriptures in this way. That prayer group now meets monthly over a Saturday breakfast and is able to offer an annual Week of Guided Prayer for local people who want to engage with it. They are encouraged by their minister, who is very supportive but deliberately does not take an active part in the group, so that it can truly be a lay ministry.

Special prayer evenings or spaces for individual prayer with different displays or objects to inspire prayer can also have a place. Offering prayer for healing requires cultural sensitivity but can be done with prayer teams or by offering prayer on a designated Sunday after Holy Communion.

The Anglican churches in Wensleydale, North Yorkshire, have worked on developing a pattern of lay-led worship so that each church in the benefice can have a service every

Sunday without relying on the presence of an ordained person. The churches ran a lay leadership course with their local Methodist partners and invited people to come on a 'no obligation' basis: that is, if they took part in the course, they did not have to commit to lead any services unless they wanted to. In the event, 16 people came on the course, and ten completed it and were prepared and willing to lead worship. Lay-led services can now happen in one church on a Sunday while the vicar leads in another church at the same time.

After the initial training, there was ongoing encourage-ment from both the vicar and the Methodist minister. They have learned that it is important to ask, 'How did it go?' and to help leaders reflect on their leading. Those who lead services are asked to prepare a 'reflection', not a sermon, and this has worked well. Some people choose to lead services with others; others prefer to lead alone.

In the beginning, the ministers encouraged 'cross-fertil-isation', with leaders moving around the churches, but it became clear that local worship leaders are best received and supported in their own church community, so that is now the accepted pattern.

When there is a fifth Sunday in a month (which usually happens four times in a year), all the churches in the benefice have lay-led services. There is no Holy Communion service that week, and usually the vicar takes a Sunday off. This is a creative solution to the real difficulty of finding clergy holiday cover in a remote area, and so the vicar plans her holidays around these services.

Once a quarter, the lay worship leaders meet to offer support to one another. Four years into this way of working, the people involved now also support one another informally outside the meetings. The response has been very positive, as most people in the benefice appreciate being able to have a service in each church every week.

Christmas and harvest services can be especially good opportunities to involve lay leaders and draw in the community—inviting a village choir to take part, for example, and asking representatives of different organisations to read or participate in other ways.

Fresh Expressions: new ways of being rural church

Café church

The same benefice has a café-style service once a month, which is lay led and organised. The vicar wrote an outline for the service and the lay leaders have made it their own. It is informal, with the congregation sitting around small tables, and coffee and cake always available. It includes singing, lectionary readings, intercessions and a reflection, which often leads into an activity. Numbers at this service vary between 19 and 65, with people of all ages joining in. The vicar comes when she is not at another service.

The café church service takes place in a traditional-style church building, which has the advantage of kitchen and toilet facilities. When the café church congregation outgrew the existing space at the back of the church, the congregation agreed to remove some pews from the south aisle to make more space and applied for a Fresh Expressions fund grant to buy some tables and chairs. There was no conflict about removing pews, because everyone could see the need. The change was driven by their vision for the café church community.

Worship has developed in this congregation, and the

café church is regarded as 'our church' by a number of the regulars. The space and style have become the setting for a Maundy Thursday supper. The culture of café church is about giving people opportunities to 'have a go' and try things out. It is not seen as a problem if something doesn't work or doesn't last: there is an understanding that all things have their season. This allows experimentation and offers a sense of ownership and belonging to all who take part.

An informal worship style makes personal sharing more natural. If it is carefully introduced, the opportunity for members of the congregation to share what God has been doing in their lives can provide encouragement and build community. Small groups gathered around tables with a tea or coffee also provide a natural setting for an interactive style of talk, with groups being asked to reflect on points made or discuss a question raised.

Working to involve all worshippers in the ownership and leading of worship needs some careful thought if the pattern and expectation is that every main Sunday service will be a celebration of Holy Communion, whether in a traditional or modern form. This limits and defines the type and amount of participation that lay people can have in the service. Congregation members can be encouraged to read lessons, lead intercessions, play music, administer the chalice and welcome and offer hospitality in many ways, but finding ways to share full responsibility for planning and organising worship and to encourage lay people to take a full part in leading the service is more of a challenge.

Where every morning service is Holy Communion, this also places limitations on mission. Communion is not an easy 'entry level' service for those seeking faith, or an accessible way for families to find a spiritual home in their local church, especially if the parents have not grown up in church. This demonstrates why it is important that any new forms of church for those who are unchurched, particularly those that take place on a different day of the week, are seen as church in their own right and not as a stepping-stone into what some see as 'proper' church.

Messy Church

Messy Church is a good example of a fresh expression as 'church in its own right'. The website describes it as 'a way of being church for families involving fun', and states that 'its values are about being Christ-centred, for all ages, based on creativity, hospitality and celebration'.[5]

A village church in County Durham had enjoyed a busy Sunday school for many years but noticed that numbers were dropping and new families were not coming to church through this event any more. Wondering what to do, they heard about a Messy Church in another village not far away. One person said, 'We thought this was another name for Sunday school, but discovered it was quite different, and we came away very inspired to start something.' The group who visited spoke warmly of the enthusiasm that they saw, and wanted to bring that enthusiasm back to their own church. Their minister was cautious in case it didn't work, but was supportive in trying Messy Church.

The organising group spent time communicating the idea of Messy Church to their congregation through articles in the newsletter and by talking to individuals. They made it clear that it would be church in its own right and not 'a way into regular Sunday services'. This message needs constant reinforcement and the group is aware that the idea is not accepted by all members of the congregation. Messy Church was advertised through the local school, toddler group and uniformed organisations. The group prayed and waited to see what would happen.

This Messy Church now meets monthly, on a Tuesday, from 3.30 to 5.30 pm. Families come straight from school, so the beginning is informal and refreshments are offered. The welcome is followed by a range of self-selected all-age activities on a theme, taken from the published Messy Church material. The activities take place in the church hall, and the group moves across the road to the church building for a 15-minute celebration at the end of the session. This gives time for the activities to be cleared and the hall reset, and they return to the hall to share a meal.

The monthly event is now an established part of the ministry of the church and involves people from the congregation. The previously reluctant minister is very happy, those who don't want to run activities or lead at the front are happy to bring or prepare food, and some of the older people have found a renewed purpose and involvement with church by joining in with Messy Church.

Forest Church

Sometimes, new forms of worship in rural areas grow out of surprising circumstances. In Grinton in Swaledale, a small congregation had a problem maintaining a large ancient building and an extensive churchyard. They started discussing what to do about cutting the overgrown grass and dealing with the bats that lived in the church building. These were not unusual problems for a rural church, but a number of things came together at the right moment, which turned the problems into an opportunity for mission and worship. Some of the church members took part in a 'Mission-Shaped

Introduction' course and were inspired to find ways to make more connections with the people in the village in which the church was set. There was also some enthusiasm for a meeting to work on the churchyard, and a group was formed. Two years on, the churchyard has become a conservation project, with bird boxes, composting, bee keeping, bat watching, scything and other related activities. The group meets monthly and it is a church project that has drawn in lots of local people who are connected to the church but not regular worshippers.

Two of those who take part are Christians who teach 'Forest Schools' locally, a way of using the environment for children's education. With their help, a 'Forest Church' activity is being developed, using the churchyard and the local rural environment for Christian worship and teaching.

Bruce Stanley, writing about Forest Church, says:

> Forest Church isn't just normal church happening outside; instead it attempts to participate with creation. We aim to learn, worship, meditate, pray and practise with the trees, at the stream, along the river edge. Participants come with an attitude of experimentation, playfulness and readiness to connect with nature. God is present in creation and can be understood through creation; you're in the sermon... The worship will happen when your heart is caught up in the beauty of the moment. Forest Church is a fresh expression of church drawing on much older traditions when sacred places and practices were outside—but also drawing on contemporary research that highlights the benefits of spending time in wild places.[6]

The Forest Church activity at Grinton includes people of all ages and is now developing into a Forest Church confirmation group, connecting with a group of young people and their parents as they explore faith and move towards confirmation. This is worship in context in a deeply rural area, where young people are used to being outside, noticing and being part of creation. Denise Owen comments, 'I sense that the connection with the land and the seasons adds to people's understanding of worship.'

A cross-cultural understanding of rural mission

The many examples in this chapter illustrate a range of Christian worship in rural areas, which fit the local context and the culture and can be owned by those who live and worship there. Rural Christian faith and worship must grow out of the soil of local culture and local experience.

'What is central to Christian worship is not "forms" but the presence of the triune God, who through his word, the Bible, enlivens, enlightens and enables all who believe in order that they may worship—serve him in spirit and in truth.'[7]

For a minister, working in a rural context often demands that they operate with a cross-cultural missional mindset. This means acting like a missionary in a foreign culture— understanding and learning to speak the heart language of the people, and so winning the right to speak of Christian faith from within the culture.

This approach is about building relationships, honouring culture, history and memory, and starting where people are in faith and life, so that they might grow into a living faith in Christ and a life of Christian worship.

Acknowledgements

Thanks to Denise Owen (an ordinand at Mirfield at the time of writing, who was made deacon in 2014) and Revd Canon Ann Chapman for their time, comments and willingness to be interviewed and quoted in this chapter.

Notes

1 Kathleen Norris, *The Cloister Walk* (Lion, 1999), p. 109
2 Paula Gooder, *Everyday God: The Spirit of the Ordinary* (Canterbury Press, 2012), p. 6
3 Ibid. p. 8
4 'Hefting' is a term used to describe sheep or cattle that belong to a particular patch of land. The animals develop an instinct from their mothers to stay in a small local area (or heft), so fences are not needed.
5 www.messychurch.org.uk
6 Bruce Stanley, *Forest Church* (Mystic Christ Press, 2013), p. 12
7 P.D. Manson, in S.B. Ferguson and D.F. Wright (eds), *New Dictionary of Theology* (IVP, 1988)

Encouraging evangelism

Simon Martin

Is evangelism possible in rural areas? Yes, it is! There does seem to be a belief, fairly widespread among some church leaders, that evangelism in rural communities is hard or even impossible. Yet some have found that, with the right approach, it can be natural and even enjoyable.

A Methodist Presbyter from the northern Yorkshire Dales tells the story of Eastertingle.

'That was great! Can we go round again?' the young boy asked. Later, several parents were overheard chatting in the local shop, with one asking the others where they had been that afternoon. 'We've been at the Methodist Chapel—it was wonderful, you should have been there.'

This was music to my ears after so much creative thought had gone into developing the Eastertingle experience that these families had just encountered. The children always enjoyed the interactive chaos that threatened to overwhelm the Christingle service. So an idea took shape to harness this chaos and enable them to experience something of the events in Jerusalem during that first Holy Week. A few children were asked to take on key roles, using a simple script printed on cards, so no rehearsal was required, and the whole building would be used to tell the Easter story.

We started with celebrations in the main chapel. Everyone shouted 'Hosanna!' enthusiastically as Jesus and his disciples walked down the aisle, entering Jerusalem. Next, we found market traders selling their wares at the front of the sanctuary; Jesus demonstrated his anger by striking their stalls so that the cardboard boxes came crashing down. Soon we heard Judas making a deal with the chief priest.

Obviously we needed to restore order from one scene to another, so I played a verse from 'He is Lord' on a recorder to mark the start of each scene. Everyone became quiet as the story unfolded. We moved into the schoolroom and ate grapes and crackers, washed down with blackcurrant squash; so we all shared in the Last Supper.

We climbed the back stairs to reach Gethsemane, then the trial took place across the chapel balcony. Pilate washed his hands as the crowd that was gathered opposite shouted for Barabbas to be freed.

As people returned to the main chapel, there was a chance to reflect and wonder what would happen next. The familiar tune of 'He is Lord' rang out through the chapel, then we heard large nails being hammered into a block of wood. Realisation dawned, along with Easter morning, and we closed with the recognition of Jesus by Mary in the garden. Jesus is alive!

But why 'Eastertingle'? Well, instead of a Christingle orange, we used a white box, with reminders of each scene placed inside—a palm leaf, chocolate coin, cracker and so on, along with an unlit candle, for each child to take home. Yet everybody knows you cannot keep God in a box: it would need to be opened and the story retold at home, amid the consumption of chocolate eggs, in the Easter holidays.

There is no avoiding the subject of evangelism. Of all the purposes of the church, Jesus chose the great commission, 'Go and make disciples', as his final word to the disciples on earth. Making disciples is therefore of prime importance and evangelism is an essential part of this process.

Evangelism starts with God and is part of our response to his goodness to us. If it feels like a duty or a burden, the place to start is on our knees, asking God to give us compassion.

At its heart, the essential elements of evangelism are straightforward—to know those without faith; to live a life different and attractive enough to invite interest; and to be able to explain our story and what the good news actually is. However, there are several reasons why evangelism can appear difficult in rural areas.

Rural communities

Many rural communities can be quite close-knit, with most people knowing much about their neighbours' lives and activities. This can make a change in life or routine, such as starting to attend church, difficult. On the other hand, some rural communities are becoming increasingly fragmented, often due to new house building or large numbers of new residents. Even for long-standing village residents, if their lives and networks of relationships are focused elsewhere, away from the community, there can be a disconnection with the place where they live. These groups are hard to contact as they do not always get involved in community events or activities, or go to the village shop or pub (if these facilities are available). In addition, the rural church is often viewed in a social or symbolic way—or even just aesthetically, primarily as a beautiful building or setting—rather than in any overtly spiritual fashion.

Rural churches

Some rural church congregations can be quite traditional in their approach, resistant to change or unwilling to speak openly about their faith, especially to people they know well. Many churches have an active and engaged presence in the community, contributing greatly to community life, but their contribution is not necessarily seen to include the active sharing of the Christian faith. In addition, the emphasis within the life of a church or group of churches may be focused mostly on regular Sunday church services. This may often be compounded by a wider view of the place of the church within the community as essentially social in nature.

The rural church can still be seen as representatively religious, acting on other people's behalf: 'Say one for me, vicar.' Yet the so-called 'death of Christendom', which includes the loosening of both formal and informal ties between rural churches and community life, is reflected in an increased alienation of rural inhabitants from even this type of vicarious faith. While there are signs of a growing interest in spiritual matters, especially among the younger generation, this may involve little engagement with traditional churches and the Christian faith as a whole, even when there are Christian elements to that spirituality.

The understanding of evangelism

Many Christians are somewhat reticent (scared stiff) concerning overt evangelism. Most may never have been involved in any form of overt evangelistic activity. Those from the older generations may have grown into faith through school and Sunday school, reflecting a process of spiritual osmosis. Alternatively, churchgoing may be assumed as a norm, with the adoption of a related lifestyle and the assembly of a set of personal beliefs and values that has led to participation in that community. Some analyses of contemporary churchgoing and religious belief describe such people as 'cultural Christians'.

For many people, evangelism is perceived to demand a radical, one-time and public identification with the Christian faith, like at a Billy Graham rally, rather than a gentle engagement over a long period of time. This assumption is likely to challenge profoundly the significance that is attached to evangelism as part of the life of the rural church. Many people have experienced confrontational or just cringeworthy attempts at evangelism in the past, which are rightly felt to be inappropriate, unhelpful and embarrassing. Examples are cited within our own research of so-called 'hit-and-run evangelists' or insensitive visiting teams; and of a serious disconnection between their involvement, approach and activities and those of rural churches, which are often left to pick up the pieces.

These comments could easily be dismissed as sweeping generalisations but their implications must be taken seriously. Rural communities collectively have long memories, and inappropriate approaches can be seriously detrimental to the current and future life of the rural church. However, there are five key issues that arise:

- Evangelism is a scary, difficult concept for many Christians.
- Most lay people in rural congregations have little or no practical experience of evangelism.
- Little or no encouragement or training in evangelism has been provided.
- Some people (including some ministers) are reluctant to engage in activities such as evangelism, which they perceive may 'rock the boat' in relation to their positive relationship with the wider local community.
- Rural ministers feel ill-equipped to either envision or equip their congregations for such activity.

The following experiences illustrate these points well. First, that of a vicar recently appointed to serve in a large group of rural churches.

Moving into rural ministry [from a large, evangelistically active new church plant], I… experienced—really for the first time—the swelling of congregations at particular times of year, the seeking out of the church for rites of passage, and the pattern of inherited forms of service and liturgy used week by week. These were small church communities accustomed to their own company, hoping that others might join and knowing that they must if the church is to survive, but demoralised by perceived disinterest and hamstrung by their inability to see how to connect.

Second, the experience of a young, active lay Methodist on moving into a rural area after graduation.

I… was shocked at the difference between the churches [in the rural circuit] and the Methodist churches I grew up in and worshipped at when at university. Not at the small (and decreasing) numbers, or even the mostly elderly congregations, but at the poverty of expectation there. Talking to some of the circuit stewards and the superintendent minister about evangelism, I was told quite firmly, 'We don't do that here, it doesn't work.' The minister said in this context, 'We do mission instead.' And then later a couple active in the largest church revealed, 'We know we ought to [share our faith] but we've no idea what to do; no one's ever shown us how.'

However, evangelism does take place in rural churches and the communities they serve. Rural churches are capable of growth in numbers, discipleship and service, including the more traditional congregations. Rural inhabitants are coming to faith, current congregations are being affirmed and revitalised, and new rural congregations and intentional Christian communities are springing into existence.

In the earlier chapter on rural mission, we made much of the importance of stories of good practice shared between rural churches. This holds equally true in the area of evangelism. However, in this case, the significance of stories goes deeper than simply discovering what other congregations have done. The telling of stories within the context of the life of the local community and the church is a valuable means of (a) envisioning and empowering ordinary congregation members to get involved in evangelism, and (b) actually drawing other members of the wider community into an attractive encounter with the Christian faith.

Evangelism as the heartbeat of the church

Journey to Faith is a free online resource on evangelism, produced by the ARC, specifically designed for rural churches. It is a training programme for rural congregations, designed to envision, empower and equip lay people and church leaders to engage in evangelism that is appropriate for their own situation in a way that is comfortable to do. Crucially, it is designed to help evangelism become part of the ongoing life of the church—a heartbeat, not a hiccup!

There is no doubt that, for most rural churches, especially small ones, evangelism can be problematic. Nevertheless, within the complex attitudes and expectations of rural congregations there is normally a recognition that evangelism is important, even if it is someone else's job to do it. This complex situation is often exacerbated by the choices made about how to engage with evangelism. For many, the solution is often to go for a 'hiccup'—a special effort, a one-off event, a bolt-on to the normal rhythm of church and community life.

In themselves, such one-off experiences are not wrong and may even be valuable and positive. However, they tend to reinforce a perception that sharing faith is done only on special occasions and that it can be safely forgotten during everyday life and the ongoing cycle of the life and ministry of the rural church. So *Journey to Faith* is designed to help rural churches make faith-sharing a natural and ongoing part of the life and experience of church members.

Evangelists or witnesses?

As a result, *Journey to Faith* deliberately chooses to use the idea of being witnesses. Some within the wider church are clearly called to be evangelists (Ephesians 4:11), with specific gifts and skills in the attractive, appropriate and persuasive communication of the gospel. But these are few in number, relative to the overall number of faithful Christians who are all called to be witnesses and share their faith with others. As 1 Peter 3:15–16 puts it, 'Always be ready to make your defence to anyone who demands from you an account of the hope that is in you; yet do it with gentleness and reverence' (NRSV).

Terminology is important. We know what evangelism is: 'sharing one's faith in Christ with the intention that someone may come to embrace the same faith' or 'sharing the good news of Christ so that others may also develop a relationship with him'. However, it may be less than helpful to carry on calling it 'evangelism', given the negative associations that this term carries for many ordinary churchgoers and for those outside the church. Suitable alternatives might be sharing faith, faith-sharing, bearing witness or being witnesses. Apart from the issue of terminology, one crucial element common to all of these alternatives is that they stress a continuous process.

Some publications and recommendations continue, per-haps without intention, to reinforce the concept that evangelism is the preserve of a skilled or specially trained minority. The view that evangelism is solely the job of local church leaders or ministers may be unwittingly reinforced, as in this from *Mosaic Evangelism*: 'One minister in Cambridgeshire looked to develop relationships in his local pub, then became chaplain of the village football team and began to have all kinds of opportunities with a group of men who would never normally have been seen dead in a church.'[1]

One result is that it might be seen as giving implicit permission for the average Christian, or even whole congregations, to absolve themselves of responsibility for faith-sharing in their own context. By contrast, the message of Paul is that the role of leaders is to enable God's people to impact the world (Ephesians 4:12), and the example of Jesus was to train his disciples, first by demonstration, then by involving them, and then by sending them out with instructions, debriefing them later (see, for example, Luke 10).

Another general misconception about what evangelism is or entails is reinforced by talking of evangelism as the initial proclamation of the faith. While evangelism may certainly be the initial communication of faith, describing it as proclamation can again be misleading. In a straw poll taken among a group of active church practitioners (mostly clergy), the majority felt that the average churchgoer would understand this to mean some sort of formal preaching, or at least a public meeting with a professional speaker or evangelist. It is important, again, to stress that these sorts of activities in themselves are not necessarily either wrong or unhelpful, but the language can marginalise the involvement of ordinary believers and narrow down the range of approaches felt to be valid in the active sharing of faith with others.

Wider experience within the rural church supports these conclusions—first, in the general impression that evangelism is primarily the preserve of the specialist or the local church leader; and, second, in the perception that evangelism primarily involves public preaching to a gathered audience or congregation (again, something that might be considered the responsibility of the vicar). One Anglican priest in the rural south-west described his experience.

> In our newly created group of five parishes, we started a discussion about evangelism as part of our overall mission. In less than five minutes an informal subgroup had convened and were discussing 'Who shall we invite to come and speak?' and 'Where can we get the most people together?' This wasn't where I had expected the discussions to start!

Intentional and unintentional evangelism

As a result of these fairly widespread attitudes and expectations, *Journey to Faith* creates a clear link between what is often now described as 'intentional' evangelism and what might be termed 'unintentional' or 'informal' evangelism. Unintentional evangelism can be understood as the low-key, ongoing witness-bearing that should be part of the congregation's heartbeat.

The same Anglican priest from the south-west revealed more.

> In subsequent discussions, it emerged that one lady in the team had, for several years, been having her neighbours round for coffee and cakes regularly, as they had asked to chat more about the things she had already shared with them. Her claim was that it seemed natural to 'talk to them about the Jesus I love'. She said later that it had started quite accidentally, literally as gossip across her hedge, and simply developed from there with more neighbours.

Journey to Faith focuses on the use of story, on the network of relationships that already exist between church members and the wider community, on the key elements of the yearly cycle of community life, and on how the rural church and its members can affirm both of these while sharing their faith in low-key and non-confrontational ways. The whole idea of being non-confrontational arose repeatedly in the ARC's research,[2] with both leaders and lay people in numerous rural churches highlighting a widespread desire to balance doing effective mission, including faith-sharing, with maintaining good relationships with the community. As one churchwarden in Herefordshire said, 'We try hard not to rock the boat too much! But some of us still recognise that the faith we are sharing does challenge people. I don't think Jesus came to make us more comfortable but to change us.'

This is why the approach of witness is so important, and why effective evangelism by rural churches is so dependent on good relationships with the community. Theologian Miroslav Volf says:

> *The bonds of affection in friendship will shape one's way of witnessing—make it respectful, considerate, and loving. The value of friendship militates against any sort of witnessing that will be deeply disrespectful and harmful of the other... Christians ought to take how they would witness to a friend to be paradigmatic of how they should witness in general.*[3]

Intentional and unintentional evangelism are two ends of a spectrum of approaches that are about the process of sharing faith. The two approaches are also intricately linked. For example, unintentional evangelism is often initiated through the witness of individuals, if encouraged and owned by a rural church or churches, and this assists with any specific plans for the conscious sharing of faith with others. Unintentional evangelism is almost entirely dependent on the bedrock of relationships and friendships between churchgoers and members of the wider community. The spectrum is illustrated by the five elements that *Journey to Faith* employs to describe how rural churches can assist people's engagement with their own journey to faith.

- **Involvement:** the low-key ways in which the churches engage with the local community, often through the relationships and friendships of churchgoers.
- **Introduction:** where elements of Christian life and faith are intentionally explained or discussed, either formally or informally.
- **Invitation:** the provision of some opportunity for people to respond to what has been shared with them—again, often via the medium of churchgoers' friendships and relationships within the wider community.
- **Induction:** welcoming the inquisitive, the newcomer or friends into a recognised relationship with the Christian family, which may ultimately include baptism and/or confirmation.
- **Instruction:** the conscious encouragement and development of faith.

The vicar of a rural church in East Anglia talks of how these elements have been developing since they started running a Messy Church two years ago.

Quite a few of our church families had children at the local primary school, and the mums particularly quickly built up friendships with others they met at the school gates. Some of these friends started coming to the drop-in coffee morning with activities for toddlers that runs twice a week, when they'd left the older children at school. Out of that came discussions about out-of-school-hours activities and we decided to start a Messy Church and get entire families on-board—even dads and partners.

So we started, and we got quite a few non-church mums (and one dad, who is a chef) involved in the Messy Church helper team. Before we knew it, we had about ten more families than we started with, invited by those who were already part of Messy Church. Our first Messy Christmas, we had 128 people, including helpers, aged nine months to 88 years.

Several families have already had their children christened in Messy Church, and one couple have asked to be 'properly' married in the church—which looks like being a specifically 'Messy Wedding'. At the request of several others, we have started a 'seekers' house group, and we are investigating 'discipleship at home' resources for some other families... including longer-standing churchgoers who are not really involved in Messy Church. One surprise was that some of the teenagers wanted to get involved, so we now have seven of them as special craft helpers. They come with their families, but can get involved, learn and develop responsibility themselves. So now we are just starting a teenagers' house group in order to help lead them on in faith and to get some of their friends involved.

There are many elements in this brief account, but there are three important aspects that relate to the 'journey' type of approach.

- The end was not seen at the beginning: things were not planned out meticulously at the start. In fact, some of the things that happened were happy accidents. A number of the church's initiatives started simply due to the responses of non-churchgoing members of the community.

- There was no clear pathway that people followed. Not everyone who was influenced had been a school-gate mum or even part of Messy Church, especially some partners.
- The five elements from *Journey to Faith* were not distinct from each other but overlapped and blended into each other, reinforcing each other in different ways. A good example of this is the house group for teenagers that developed from helping with Messy Church.

Churches as evangelism's heartbeat

Pope Francis, in the groundbreaking *Evangelii Gaudium* (2013), talks of the vital role of the parish in reaching out to communities.

The parish is not an outdated institution, precisely because it possesses great flexibility... While certainly not the only institution which evangelises, if the parish proves capable of self-renewal and constant adaptivity, it continues to be 'the Church living in the midst'... This presumes that it really is in contact with the homes and lives of people, and does not become a useless structure out of touch with people or a self-absorbed group made up of a chosen few... In all its activities the parish encourages and trains its members to be evangelisers.[4]

Pope Francis here recognises and reinforces the importance of the local church and its members in effective evangelism, strengthening and encouraging the conviction that it is not simply individual Christians who bear witness, but the whole body of Christ.

Every case study and example in this chapter highlights the role of rural churches in encouraging and enabling evangelism in rural situations. The main players in evangelism are the Christians who are already resident and active within rural communities. There is a place for special events, for the involvement of outside specialists and speakers, and being part of a national initiative such as 'Hope' or Back to Church Sunday, but the most effective means of sharing faith is through words and deeds by people who are known within the community.

Evangelism is one part of the overall mission of the church. As some of the examples have already illustrated, it is often impossible to make clear distinctions between how and where rural churches engage in any of the Five Marks of Mission (see 'Mission in rural contexts' earlier in this book). In particular, it may be difficult and perhaps even unhelpful, given the complex ways in which people journey to faith, to separate evangelism from discipleship.

Using 'Journey to Faith'

A curate from a large group of rural churches in Yorkshire tells how they ended up using *Journey to Faith* not once but twice.

It was an experiment, simply because I knew one of the people who had designed the course. I got permission to run it for three of our parishes, to be offered over two consecutive Saturday mornings. There was considerable suspicion to start with, so we suggested that people just turned up to the first session as a taster—with the bribe of lunch together in the pub afterwards and first-class coffee during it!

The thing that I noticed immediately was that it gave those who came the opportunity to do two things that we are not normally very good at. Firstly, to actually discuss things properly with each other. There was just enough input to guide discussion, but with open-ended questions, value attached to contributors' opinions and no specifically right answers, which helped things greatly. In our case, to be honest, it was good that it was only me running it. If the vicar had been there that first day, I'm sure people would have felt less free to talk, share and ask questions... perhaps anticipating and expecting that the vicar would tell them the answers. Then it was good to be involved in activities—which were both fun and instructive—again without everything (or even much at all) being done from the front.

The most valuable thing of all was the emphasis throughout on stories, and how different stories all fit together. [In fact, the first session is called 'We're all part of the story'.] Everyone had the opportunity to think through and discuss various stories with which they were involved: my story, the Jesus story, our church story, God's story and experimenting with ways of telling a story of their own faith journey. It is one of the gentlest introductions to personal witnessing I've come across.

At the end of the first session, we all had the opportunity to think about the many ways in which people come into contact with the Christian faith. In other words, there is no single right way, and conversion (which is a tough idea for many to swallow) is most frequently a process, both complex and messy—and there are many entry points, which seldom start with overt belief. This was very valuable, as it gave people freedom to accept both their own complex faith stories and the numerous ways they interact quite naturally with people currently outside the church family.

I thought the session was good, and the nine people who attended obviously thought so, too. The following Saturday morning they all returned, along with twelve others who had been persuaded to join in but hadn't been there for the first session. As a result, I agreed to run the two-part course again the following fortnight, for all who wanted to come but had missed the very first session. By then, we had 16 for the second run-through. So out of three parishes, with about 60 regular, active churchgoers, nearly half completed the training. Marvellous!

But what have we done with all this? Some things have developed from the practical suggestions and activities included in the second session; some has arisen from the imaginations of the participants themselves. Not a single thing has been initiated by me, although I have provided as much support and assistance as I can in getting things off the ground in the six months since the courses were run.

Some people have worked together to draw up a yearly cycle of all the events, activities and occasions within the communities and the churches, so we can see all the opportunities that exist where we can be more involved with community activities. This was the focus of another morning we had together, about two months after the end of the second course. One side-effect is that the three churches are working together on these things.

One parish is adding a coffee-and-croissants café-style service once a month (as a trial), with an informal come-and-go approach, having a focus not on structured worship but on a time to ask and share questions for discussion. We will probably start using a resource called 'Table Talk' for this. If it goes well, the service may become more frequent.

In the largest of the parishes there are plans in hand to take the church out into the village, by using some celebrations from the liturgical calendar, actively including members of the community and celebrating outside the church building. We will be doing this with a Harvest service, which seemed an obvious, popular place to begin, combining it with the long-standing village harvest supper, and we've been asked to provide an after-supper speaker.

Perhaps least noticeably, but most significantly, some churchgoers are finding the courage to tell their stories to their neighbours, without any big song-and-dance or unrealistic expectations. One elderly couple have started attending church for the first time in nearly 25 years, 'because our next-door neighbour invited us after we had got talking about why we stopped going to church after the death of our daughter'. Another lady confided to me recently, 'Once I broke the ice, it has been really quite enjoyable talking to people about what matters to me and to them—even people I've known for decades. It is still hard to talk directly about Christ, but much easier to say what motivates me and what a difference my own faith has made to my life.'

Now the rest of the churches in the group have asked if we can run the courses with them as well.

Journey to Faith is not a panacea for evangelism in rural areas, and there have been occasions when it has not been so successful. However, it remains the only resource designed specifically with rural, especially small, churches in mind. You can find all the resources and material for *Journey to Faith* at www.germinate.net/go/evangelism. There is also a summary and an evaluation of a small number of resources and training materials from elsewhere, that have also been found useful in encouraging rural evangelism. If you feel encouraged to dip your toe into evangelism in your own rural location, there is plenty of help available.

Notes

1 Roger Standing, *Mosaic Evangelism: Sharing Jesus with a multi-faceted society* (Grove Books Ev102, 2013), p. 26

2 Simon Martin, *Resourcing and Training for the Rural Church: Mapping the experience of contemporary practitioners and churchgoers* (Arthur Rank Centre, 2011). www.germinate.net/go/mappingreport

3 See www.facebook.com/miroslav.volf.12/posts/299347876779169

4 Apostolic Exhortation *Evangelii Gaudium* of the Holy Father Francis (2013), II.28. http://w2.vatican.va/content/francesco/en/apost_exhortations/documents/papa-francesco_esortazione-ap_20131124_evangelii-gaudium.html

Fresh expressions of church

Simon Martin

What are fresh expressions of church?

A fresh expression is a form of church for our changing culture, established primarily for the benefit of people who are not yet members of any church.[1]

'Fresh expressions' is one name for innovative forms of church that have a strong focus on mission. Other labels have been used, such as emerging church, new forms of church, new ways of being church and church plants.[2]

You will almost certainly already have heard of the term 'fresh expressions of church' and the *Mission-Shaped Church* report, out of which the Fresh Expressions movement has developed. As the numbers of fresh expressions present in the countryside increases, it is important to recognise the key intentions of this new approach and what part it can play in the mission and ministry of the rural church.

The primary aim of fresh expressions is to reach people outside the existing church. They have a fourfold emphasis on:

- serving those outside church
- listening to people and entering their culture
- making discipleship a priority
- forming church

On this basis, a fresh expression should be:

- missional, going out to people who are not already church members
- relevant and appropriate for those at whom it is aimed (which includes the need to listen deeply and respond)
- educational, helping those who come to learn more about God, faith and the church
- aiming to grow into a group of people that worships God as its primary purpose, rather than simply being another social group

Fresh expressions are about creating a welcoming, engaging space where faith can be shared and worship can take place.

Many rural churches are deeply engaged in community life and activity. However, it can no longer be assumed that there is automatic participation in the life of a village by those that live there. Residents of the countryside are also part of a modern culture with networks of relationships and social activity that are not based on a specific place, people or shared values. One experienced minister in the rural north-east says:

Rural ministry today... has to be approached cross-culturally. Fewer and fewer cultural and spiritual values are shared between church and society, and there is decreasing engagement with Christian faith or the life of existing churches. We can no longer assume that we automatically know what rural communities and individuals are like, and we certainly cannot assume people's familiarity with Christian basics. We have to find out, and approach them on their terms.

Fresh expressions of church are supported by an organisation called Fresh Expressions,[3] which provides resources, ideas and training. The organisation Fresh Expressions has identified a range of different types of fresh expression (and has also identified activities that are not genuine fresh expressions). The different types are as follows:

- **Existing congregation renewal:** the renewal of an existing congregation through careful listening to the non-churchgoers whom the congregation is called to serve.
- **Reinventing an existing group:** an existing fringe group, mission project or community service is reinvented so that it is no longer a stepping-stone to Sunday church, but becomes church in its own right.
- **Creating a new community:** creating a new Christian community within a church, parish, benefice or circuit, as a mission initiative.
- **A large mission initiative:** an initiative that covers several groups of churches, across one or more circuits, deaneries or other groupings.

Rural examples of all of these can be found, with *Mission-Shaped and Rural* by Sally Gaze providing a useful handbook of early case studies across the range.

Fresh expressions are intended to be a journey

The following diagram represents the process that a fresh expression may take as it is created and develops into a worshipping community. It is frequently described as a journey.[4]

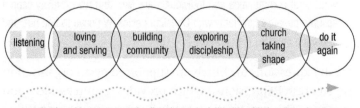

underpinned by prayer, ongoing listening and relationship with the wider church

A fresh expression is assumed to begin by listening to people outside the church in order to discern the best way to love and serve them. A further unspoken assumption is that whatever develops as a result of listening will be different from anything that the pre-existing churches are already doing. From the practical evidence of love and service it is intended that a new community of some sort will be created—including both those who started the fresh expression and those who have been drawn in. At some point, often very early on, this community will intentionally explore discipleship together in forms appropriate for those with no experience of traditional church. As the community grows in its knowledge and understanding of being together in Christ, it will take on its own basic ecclesial characteristics, rather than adopting a traditional form. Ideally, the community will itself encourage its members to repeat the process with others outside the boundaries of traditional church.

Fresh expressions are intended to be genuinely church

Church Army has developed a set of indicators that help define a fresh expression within the Anglican tradition: *What is an Anglican Fresh Expression of Church? 10 indicators.*[5] Most of the indicators are also applicable to any denomination. Deciding if a fresh expression has become or is developing into a church is helpful in order to ensure that the journey is continuing beyond the initial inception of the fresh expression. These six questions are helpful to consider:

- Has something Christian and communal been started that is new, rather than an existing group that has been modified or rebadged?

- Has the starting group tried to engage with non-church-goers? Is there an intention to create a fresh expression of church, not simply an outreach project from an existing church?
- Is there intention to become church? The key is that the fresh expression is not seen as a bridge back to what might be thought of as 'real church'.
- Do the majority of members, who are part of the public gathering, see this as their major or only participation in church?
- Is there aspiration to live out the four creedal marks of church: one, holy, catholic and apostolic? In other words, is the group offering fellowship (one); growing towards God (holy); part of the whole body of Christ, the wider church (catholic); and seeking to share faith (apostolic)?
- Does the resultant community meet at least once a month? This is considered to be the minimum needed to ensure continuity, while building up a sense of commitment and discipleship.

The organisation Fresh Expressions makes it clear that the aim of a fresh expression 'is not to provide a stepping stone into existing church, but to form new churches in their own right'.[6]

George Fisher, Director of Mission in Lichfield Diocese, illustrates this: 'Last week I went to visit… one of our fresh expressions, and on the wall was written by one of the mums, "This is my church. 'Normal' church is too much for me—I couldn't handle that. But here we still do praying and stuff. This is my kind of place."' A pioneer Methodist minister from rural Cornwall talks of 'being church for those who don't do church'.

The ideal and the real

There are significant issues surrounding fresh expressions of church that raise doubts for some rural church practitioners. Some of these concerns are not exclusive to the rural context, but others are. Most of the issues revolve around the nature and identity of fresh expressions, the relationship they have with traditional (inherited) church, the fact that many rural churches are small and the fact that most exist in multi-church groups. These issues reflect tensions between the ideal and the reality.

Recent research highlights confusion over what is actually a fresh expression of church. In 2013, the Church Army Research Unit studied 1124 examples of new approaches to church, from ten Anglican dioceses. Over half were found not to meet the criteria of a fresh expression as the term has 'been borrowed and used indiscriminately since 2004'.[7]

There are often questions about the relevance of fresh expressions of church in rural contexts and, perhaps, some misunderstanding of how the term is used and what it is used to describe. One regular participant at a café church described it as 'a family service with croissants and good coffee and not much different from anything that a more traditional church with mission aspirations might do'. He questioned why it was called a fresh expression at all. Some fresh expressions have a desire to be separate from what traditional churches are doing, but they are actually not very different, either in composition or in ethos. Other fresh expressions do what they do with firm and friendly links with their parent churches. At the same time, some quite traditional rural churches are doing very similar missional activities without any reference to fresh expressions.

Research reveals that continuing popular assumptions about a largely urban or suburban location for most fresh expressions of church are mistaken.[8] So, in the deeply rural Diocese of Norwich it may not be surprising that, in 2012, 44 per cent of all fresh expressions were in specifically rural locations. However, more significant is the combined data from ten Anglican dioceses across a spectrum from very rural (Norwich) to urban (Liverpool). This revealed that, by 2012, over 28 per cent of all fresh expressions were to be found in rural areas. This represents the largest growth in fresh expressions for any geographical location. Thus the figures for the Church of England, at least, suggest that fresh expressions are finding increasing relevance in rural circumstances. Research of a different sort highlights the perceived relevance of fresh expressions approaches for the rural Methodist Church.[9]

Norman Ivison, from the organisation Fresh Expressions, has attempted to dispel some common myths that contribute to confusion about what is and is not a fresh expression of church and what you have to do or be to start one.

- You don't have to be part of a large, urban or suburban congregation for a fresh expression to be effective.
- A large team is not needed to start a fresh expression.
- Fresh expressions are not only relevant to those from the evangelical tradition.
- Every fresh expression is different. They are not clones of one particular approach; nor are they an attempt to squeeze new Christian communities into a specific mould.
- New fresh expressions do not simply imitate what others are already doing elsewhere; all are contextually appropriate, relevant to the people they are trying to serve.

- Fresh expressions do not aim to get new people to go to traditional church.
- It is not possible to start a fresh expression only through worship, as this will not create a community.

Other research revealed a ready desire among a broad sample of rural Anglican benefices to start a fresh expression of church, with several groups identifying this as a development they wanted to take forward. This overall picture is supported by our own experience of numerous individual rural examples. Fresh expressions have a very real place in rural contexts.

Nevertheless, a priest in rural North Yorkshire suggests that small and multiple rural churches have their limits:

It will not work if you are asking old, tired people from small, already overworked churches in deeply rural places to find some more energy to put into another programme. [What] would make a difference would be to bring new and different energy and... [more] people from outside to impact these places. Otherwise it is just another initiative that we have to resource [entirely] ourselves from an already limited and overstretched pool.

Some have expressed concern about creating new small congregations in addition to the pre-existing small local congregations, especially if the groups do not relate to each other or the existing village churches. As a result, fresh expressions can be perceived as unhelpful, drawing people away from already small churches, when in fact they are aiming to reach out to those who would not otherwise engage with church.

It is recognised by many rural church leaders that, to create a critical mass of people to start, maintain and benefit from a fresh expression, most would have to operate across more than one church or a group of churches. This approach can lead to strengthening links and high-quality collaboration across churches of the same or different denominations and enable more efficient use of limited resources and personnel. However, unless a strong group identity already exists, such new initiatives are hard to maintain beyond the community where the activity takes place. A frequent comment is 'It's very hard to get people from one village to be enthused about what's going on in the next village.' The absence of collegiality in many rural groups with congregations that focus purely on their own church can make the development of a fresh expression—or, indeed, any new initiative—much more challenging.

Pure... or mixed?

The phrase 'mixed economy' has been developed to describe and emphasise the way different forms of church can exist alongside each other in a relationship of mutual respect and support. This terminology was first used by Rowan Williams and helps describe the situation in many places, including rural areas, where fresh expressions of church exist alongside traditional church (sometimes called inherited church). The language of the mixed economy 'has proved immensely helpful in assisting people to see that the traditional and new forms of church are not in competition but complementary'.[10] This complementarity is necessary for the sake of the gospel and our discernment of God's mission.

Our own recent research[11] shows that rural fresh expressions, and the approach they represent, are often closely linked to existing churches (traditional/inherited). This is confirmed by both Revd Sally Gaze and Pete Atkins, who lead the national Fresh Expressions Rural Round Table and say that 'rural fresh expressions work much more closely with inherited/traditional forms of church than do urban or suburban examples'. A Baptist advocate of fresh expressions speaks out of substantial experience of rural mission and ministry: 'Care is needed to demonstrate that the new can be grown without the necessity for changing or getting rid of the old.'

We suggest that the rural church is the natural home of the mixed economy. Rural fresh expressions almost always develop organically alongside traditional rural churches. Whether an activity, initiative or group is or is not a fresh expression is almost irrelevant, as the vision, ethos and approach offered by Fresh Expressions are helping to revitalise mission in rural churches. Rural Christians are engaging deeply with local community and cultures, previously unreached people are coming to a living faith, disciples are being nurtured and Christian communities are being multiplied and grown.

'Mission-Shaped Introduction' (MSI)

The Fresh Expressions organisation has created a training resource to introduce churches to the ideas and methods of fresh expressions. *Mission-Shaped Introduction* (MSI)[12] explores how a fresh expression is an alternative way of thinking, not just a new model of church to be copied. It is a mindset that starts not with church but with people who don't belong to church. As one rural lay person with extensive training experience concludes: '[It] is an excellent tool for rural churches as it emphasises a change of mindset, identifies key areas where this is needed, and outlines some very practical and relevant steps by which this can be achieved.'

The course comprises five major sessions of input, inter-action, discussion and reflection, and a final forward-looking session.

1 Rediscovering mission: the mission of God as the foundation of the church
2 Changing world, changing church: how the church might respond to a changing world
3 Reimagining community
4 Reimagining worship
5 Reimagining discipleship and leadership
6 Where do we go from here?

MSI is intended to be run locally (for example, within a single group of churches, circuit or deanery). There is no compulsion to start a fresh expression of church as a result or to enrol people for further training, but it has the potential to challenge thinking about mission, community, discipleship, worship and leadership.

One important emphasis for rural churches that MSI lacks, but which is recognised by the Fresh Expressions team, relates to church buildings. These have an essential place in the thinking of many rural churches and communities, which can cause a serious stumbling-block when talking about doing things differently. Issues concerning church buildings can easily come to dominate consideration of the mission of any rural church. Helpful initial thoughts on how buildings might be incorporated into a fresh expressions approach can be found in the section of Chapter 6 in Sally Gaze's *Mission-Shaped and Rural* entitled 'Shrines and slide rules—towards a mission perspective on church buildings'.

Case studies

There are numerous examples of fresh expressions of church being developed in rural areas. Some of these case studies identify themselves as a fresh expression and are recognised as such, yet most do not meet all the fundamental criteria for a fresh expression. By contrast, others do not explicitly describe themselves as a fresh expression but include many of the indicators identified as essential, and some others have been labelled as fresh expressions by others. Here are just a few of the many good examples present in rural areas.

Men in the Pub

One of the more frequently identified rural fresh expression are groups for men that offer something very different from regular church services. Revd Graham Hedger talks of his experience in Suffolk.

'I'm off down the pub with the vicar.' Who would deny their nearest and dearest a night out at the local in the company of the vicar? It all started as a chance remark between me and one of the churchwardens, about how we might reach some of the local men who helped do things for the church but rarely, if ever, attended a service. A venue where men could meet and chat about a range of issues was required... and 'Men in the Pub' was born. The landlord opened the kitchen especially for the group. It meant extra business for him on a normally quiet night, and the attraction of real ale, local cider and home-cooked food has proved a great draw.

Looking back, we knew we wanted a neutral venue for men to meet and a forum where men could talk about the issues that affected them. (In my experience, men seldom 'open up' when women are present.) An evangelistic meeting with speakers would have driven many away. Instead, the format of a pint, a meal and a good chat between neighbours was what was needed. We spread the news by word of mouth, and on the first evening 18 men turned up. Soon the air was filled with chat—men who hadn't previously talked openly about faith chatting away about Christianity, or faith in the world of work.

It has helped us build relationships with those on the edge of the church and beyond, and the group has gone from strength to strength. We meet every three months; over the past 18 months our lowest attendance has been twelve and our highest 21. Not everyone comes all the time but around 25 men have attended. Of these, under half come to church regularly, with the rest divided between occasional attenders and non-attenders.

Contrary to the ideals of the Fresh Expressions movement, in many cases these sorts of groups assume they will help increase men's involvement in traditional church. Certainly, in this example, there is no current plan to create a brand new congregation from Men in the Pub. However, a new community has been created, people who were previously unreached by the church have been welcomed, and the meetings take place on their territory and in their culture. Traditional aspects and approaches to church are not forced on them, and there is a strong intention to encourage faith development. Is it a fresh expression of church? It is certainly 'fresh' and it is certainly an 'expression of church' but best described as one closely linked to a pre-existing church that is demonstrating a heart for mission.

Parish Praise at Willand

Another common form of rural fresh expression involves new approaches to worship that seek the most appropriate ways of engaging with people alienated from traditional church. Here is one example from Canon Anna Norman-Walker in Devon.

A key issue facing St Mary's, Willand, was that its congregation was made up of those who lived in the old part of the village, and the church was functioning as though it existed to minister only to the 'old village'. Willand has two large new housing developments but the church was barely making any contact with those who lived there or were new to the village. The priority was to find ways of reaching out to the newer community while continuing to embrace the old village and the existing congregation.

The single most important strategic decision was not to alter the traditional 11.00 service but to introduce, in parallel with it, a new weekly family service—Parish Praise—which would reach out to the community beyond the old village and 'old village' culture.

St Mary's church building offered too many restrictions and the traditional 11.00 am service was simply not attracting families from the village. The decision was made to use the church hall for a 9.30 am Parish Praise each Sunday, driven by the desire to provide a worship opportunity for families and young children without the constraints of traditional expectations. The hall is used for lots of weekday events so people are already at home in it.

At Parish Praise you are welcome regardless of background, beliefs, doubts and uncertainties. Asking questions is part of the culture and two midweek discussion groups have quickly sprung up out of this ethos… 'exploring Christianity' and 'open to questions'. We try not to broker certainty at Parish Praise but to foster wonder, nurture faith and encourage growth.

As a result, over a four-year period, the overall church family doubled in size.

> What was particularly exciting was that the growth the church experienced was mostly among the unchurched and young families. After ten years with no organised children's ministry, the church began to draw an average of 25 children and young people, [while] two holiday clubs were hosted that attracted around 50 children from the surrounding rural area.

Once Parish Praise had been running for 18 months, a united service in church was introduced—a monthly coming together of the two congregations for a Common Worship Holy Communion, with a light touch. The cost was that some of the very committed members of the 11.00 congregation stayed away because they did not like the Common Worship liturgy, and some of the Parish Praise congregation stayed away because they did not like worshipping in a church building. However, the service attracted 80–100 people, and those who stayed away continued to participate on other Sundays. This was considered to be a 'price worth paying to keep the church members together as a family'. It also helped to give long-established church members a glimpse of the growth of the wider church, which turned out to be a great encouragement. Anna recalls how one 87-year-old member of the original congregation said, with tears in her eyes, how wonderful it was to see children in the church again.

Here a new community has been formed through Parish Praise. For some, perhaps many, of its members, this has genuinely become church as they develop faith and grow in their Christian journey. But, despite its difference in many ways from the traditional church at St Mary's, there was never any intention that Parish Praise should be separate from it. Considerable effort has been put in, and sacrifices made, to ensure that both congregations see themselves as part of a single church family.

Little Fishes in Wiltshire

Revd Philip Bromiley, Associate Missioner for Fresh Expressions in Salisbury Diocese, tells this story.

Little Fishes is a parent-and-toddler group in one of five parishes in the Oldbury Benefice. Every time the group gathers, it seems to take on more of the characteristics of church.

We began in 2008 with six children, their parents and three volunteers. It was founded on a prayerful vision to meet the needs of isolated parents in our rural communities. The group risked being explicitly Christian in approach and ethos, even though they were seeking to appeal to those having little contact with church. After a year, the group had grown so much that a larger village hall was needed. Now there are about 35 children... plus parents.

Meetings begin with welcome and a prayer. After a short Bible story, the children move into an activity based on that story. Snack time ensues and then Christian children's songs are sung around a guitar. The group has produced some godly fruit, indicating that it is more than simply a parent-and-toddler group. One family approached to enquire about baptism. When I reached for the diary to choose a Sunday, they said, 'Oh no, we want it on a Wednesday morning, because Little Fishes is our church.'

We pray for people. On one occasion, we were deeply saddened to hear that one mum had a baby born with a terminal illness. For three months we all prayed for the family and sang 'He's got the little tiny baby in His hands'. Many from the group attended the funeral in church and sang our Little Fishes songs. There is also an impressive standard of mutual pastoral care, whether through bereavement, divorce or the everyday challenges of parenthood. Recently, we re-enacted the Last Supper as the daily Bible story. Everyone ate bread that had been made together, though some refused the blackcurrant squash on offer. There was a real sense of togetherness. Is Little Fishes emerging as a church?

137

Cook@Chapel in Hanslope

Katharine Crowsley, from Hanslope Methodist Chapel, tells how she has been working with a growing group of rural teenagers.

Five years ago I felt that the church didn't have much for children aged eleven, twelve and into their teenage years. I thought there was a real need to reach out to young people within the village context and work with them. There seemed to be an assumption that maybe, at twelve, children would leave the church, and most weren't involved or connected with the church at all.

I cottoned on to the idea of using food as a way of reaching out, particularly to young people. In my day job I'm a teacher and I'm aware that many young people don't have much opportunity to cook at school, and lots of families don't sit down and eat a meal together. So I thought the idea of cooking and sharing food would be a good starting point.

Initially, we found the young people coming and joining Cook@Chapel for a bit... and then moving on. But after a couple of years they came and they stayed, and we saw more of a small community of young people starting to grow up. What we have now is a group of young people who've been involved for about two years with the small missional community that's building here. More and more have joined—eight in the past year. Some come from a church background, and they're quite confident within the development of their faith, but many come from a background where they've not been involved with church at all.

Sometimes conversations about spirituality come up quite naturally while we're cooking and preparing the food. For example, when we were making pizza dough we'd talk about the parable of the yeast. Some of those conversations come up really naturally. But we've also tried to introduce times of prayer into Cook@Chapel—which seems to have fitted very naturally as well. We've tried lots of different activities but one in particular has really stuck.

We have a big mixing bowl and the young people put their prayers into the bowl and then pass it round from one to the other, reading out the prayers as they go. It is really positive that what started as a one-off activity, which wasn't going to be repeated, has ended as something the young people want to do again and again—getting the bowl and carrying out this 'mixing bowl of prayer' every week. It forms a key focus of the worship time of our group.

Katharine goes on to discuss avoiding Christian jargon, developing holistic faith in small steps, involving the older youngsters in leadership and planning, starting to serve the wider community, sharing faith with others, and working as a team. She is now offering this expertise to other churches and communities, so that they can adapt it to fit their own unique circumstances. Cook@Chapel is one rural example that appears to fulfil all of Fresh Expression's underlying ideals.

If you wish to explore more about fresh expressions of church in rural contexts, there is a growing list of examples and case studies, with links to websites and articles about them, on the ARC website at www.germinate.net/go/ruralfx. You will also find links to a wider range of material related to rural fresh expressions. The *Mission-Shaped Ministry* course is evaluated in depth from a rural perspective at www.germinate.net/go/ruralmsm.

Notes

1 www.freshexpressions.org.uk/about/whatis
2 www.freshexpressions.org.uk/guide/about/whatis/unpacking
3 www.freshexpressions.org.uk
4 www.freshexpressions.org.uk/guide/develop
5 www.churcharmy.org.uk/Publisher/File.aspx?ID=138340
6 www.freshexpressions.org.uk/about/whatis
7 *An Analysis of Fresh Expressions of Church and Church Plants Begun in the Period 1992–2012* (Church Army Research Unit, 2013), p. 82. www.churchgrowthresearch.org.uk/UserFiles/File/Reports/churchgrowthresearch_freshexpressions.pdf
8 Ibid. p. 33
9 P. Rolph, J. Rolph and J. Cole (2011). 'Methodist Fresh Expressions: Listening to leaders of specific rural initiatives in England' in *Rural Theology*, New Series Issue 9, Part 2 (2011), pp.129–142
10 Steven Croft, 'What counts as a fresh expression of church and who decides?' in Martyn Percy and Louise Nelstrop (eds), *Evaluating Fresh Expressions: Explorations in emerging church* (Canterbury Press, 2008), p. 5
11 Simon Martin, *Resourcing and Training for the Rural Church: Mapping the experience of contemporary practitioners and churchgoers* (Arthur Rank Centre, 2011). www.germinate.net/go/mappingreport
12 www.freshexpressions.org.uk/missionshapedintro

Children and young people

Rona Orme

Wherever your footsteps touch the earth, a rich harvest is gathered. Desert pastures blossom, and mountains celebrate. Meadows are filled with sheep and goats; valleys overflow with grain and echo with joyful songs.

PSALM 65:11–13 (CEV)

Growing up 'rural'

Children develop in the same way the world over, but where they live affects their experiences and their life chances. Some children love growing up in a small community where they are known by their neighbours. They may enjoy plenty of space and perhaps the freedom to roam outside. Others will be frustrated by the lack of children in their age group, having to take a bus to school and the poor mobile phone coverage and internet speed. The drawbacks are likely to increase as they grow. Lack of transport can limit the amount of time young people spend with their friends in a way that is incomprehensible to their urban and suburban peers.

There are similar strengths and weaknesses for children and young people who attend a small rural church. They may appreciate being well known and cherished among the few children in a congregation, or they may find that experience limiting or overwhelming. Sunday school may happen just once or twice a month because there are insufficient leaders or children to justify the effort, and it is likely to include children from one to twelve years old in the same group. Traditional ways of working with children in church seem to fade away when numbers are few, although some activities find new energy and life when there is an influx of families to a village through the building of new homes or when houses pass to a new generation.

One of the strengths of village life can be the strong sense of community. St Mary's, Badby, in Northamptonshire, has tapped into this sense of belonging to develop a number of activities. Remembrance is an important commemoration in the village. With all ages working together, the church has researched the stories of the men whose names appear on the war memorial and then invited a serving soldier to talk at the service of Remembrance about his experiences in Afghanistan. This focus of interest has taken the congregation out into the community while making sure that children and young people understand the experience of previous generations.

Unlike people in suburban areas, rural residents may identify strongly with 'their' church even if they rarely attend. This can mean that invitations to services such as Back to Church Sunday may be met with puzzlement. A better approach, and one that readily involves children and young people, may be to organise an annual pet service, where the initial invitation may seem to be more for the pets than the people. Relationships can then be built that help people feel welcome in church. Another idea is to run all-age occasions in which Bible stories are shared and explored, but with a strong emphasis on hospitality. All Saints Church, Pytchley, in Northamptonshire, runs a monthly event called Friday Family Fun, which takes place after school with activities and food for all ages from birth to 90+. Pizza Praise, organised by the Astwick Vale Benefice in south Northamptonshire, is a similar idea that links worship and Bible input with the eating of pizza together by all ages on a Sunday afternoon.

Nationally, research shows that the proportion of children and young people who take part in worship increasingly do so midweek rather than on a Sunday. This is partly because families have other activities to pursue on Sundays and partly because traditional Sunday services do not attract them. Some churches are reluctant to change what they usually offer on Sundays to welcome a broader group of people, when they have no guarantee of success. If this is the case, it becomes easier to develop something new and, perhaps, more relevant in a different slot. Sutton, a tiny village west of Peterborough, developed a brief, informal all-age service at 9.15 am to encourage families to attend worship before heading out to sports training or family activities.

Play and Praise

Di Woolridge is a lay pioneer minister who has developed a weekly 'Play and Praise' worship service for the under-fives at St Lawrence's Church, Gnosall, Staffordshire. Her initial idea was to build closer relationships with families who had brought their children for baptism, after a parent pointed out that the church made no particular provision for the age group. It is not a playgroup but a time of worship devised for younger children and their parents or carers. Di explains:

In terms of format, we have between 30 and 40 minutes of worship before the children get on with some art and craft activities associated with the theme of the service. It is quite structured and follows a traditional church pattern of liturgy. This usually includes an opening prayer with a song (usually with accompaniment from the children on percussion instruments), the lighting of a candle, a couple of songs (usually in the New Wine style of children's worship, with actions where possible), followed by a Bible story, more songs and a final blessing.

We also have a collection (something that came from the parents who asked if they could give), an interactive grace (such as the one used by Messy Church), notices and time to remember people's birthdays, followed by arts and crafts while parents have a well-earned tea break.

When we started Play and Praise, we had five children and three parents coming along. Three years on, we are averaging around 18 children and twelve adults. We have about 30 children on the books in all. Some come every week without fail; most come three out of every four weeks and others come occasionally. We don't stop for school holidays at all because it's a worship service. Other services in the church don't stop simply because it isn't term time and I have insisted that we keep going too, so Play and Praise meets 50 weeks a year. The only times we miss are Holy Week (though we do hold a special event on Good Friday for families, including the Play and Praise families) and the week between Christmas and New Year.

Many churches only offer something like Play and Praise during term time, but people appreciate the regularity and look forward to it as one of the highlights of the week. I'd say it's really important to look at how such things are set up in the first place and what the intention and the values are. We are a village of about 350 families. We have found that we no longer need to advertise Play and Praise because families tell others about it. The health visitor and others, such as the local preschool, refer people to us.

I've got a good team to help with it all now. I now alternate the running of Play and Praise with the rector, and others from the Sunday congregations are involved on a rota basis. It has brought in people we weren't expecting. For instance, some congregation members who tend to go to 7.45 am Holy Communion have come along to help, and that's wonderful.

We have a Facebook Play and Praise page and it's great to see how

144

the mums connect with that all the time, commenting on what has been happening and even asking each other to pray for particular situations or illnesses in their families. Other developments that have come out of Play and Praise are Yummy Mummies (a monthly coffee morning and discussion group for young mums, where we use 'Table Talk' material[1] to stimulate discussion) and a monthly support group for mums with anxiety issues. We have also recently started a house group for those who want to look a bit deeper at the Christian faith for themselves.[2]

Involving men: Who Let The Dads Out?

One way in which rural is no different from urban is that parent-and-baby or parent-and-toddler groups often seem to cater more for mums than dads. A number of Who Let The Dads Out? groups have developed to provide a great space for dads and male carers to spend time with their small children.[3] These monthly gatherings are a good way for churches to build relationships with men while encouraging family life. Most Who Let The Dads Out? groups meet on a Saturday morning so that as many men as possible, including dads who do not live with their children, can attend. They usually offer bacon butties and newspapers for the men, free play for the children and a craft activity.

Bev Theobald is Deputy Head of the infant school in Mulbarton, a growing village of around 3000 near Norwich. She started a half-termly Who Let The Dads Out? group.

I started by running a one-off school summer term event for dads and kids and was challenged to consider doing it more often. I approached the church for support and backing and found that the vicar and several parishioners were highly supportive. We now run the group in the infant school and typically we get around 20 dads and 30 children.

I subsequently found out about Who Let The Dads Out? through the Diocese of Norwich and was really pleased to be able to connect into the movement.

I think the school link and school location are key for our attendance. A couple of our helping dads are from the church, but the majority who come are linked to the school. This makes advertising easy and the dads are not threatened by the environment they are coming into. Not surprisingly, most of the children are infant age, although we do get one or two preschoolers and some junior-school-age siblings.

The group has definitely helped to build community in the village. Although there is a strong community built around the village football club, this isn't for everyone, and our group helps to form other dad-to-dad connections. It helps the school significantly as we get to know the dads of some of our children much better. Mulbarton is a growing village so this group also helps new families in the village to get connected. One of our main helpers is a chef so our core activity is cooking. All our children and dads get to cook something together each time we meet, and they love this part of the session.

It is harder to say specifically how we support families. We have a couple of single dads who come, who have weekend access to their children. The group is a great place for them to be able to come. It supports them as dads and helps them to have a memorable time with their children, strengthening those bonds.

One of the big challenges is how we help to connect church and community together. Our evangelistic approach is based on getting alongside the dads and just going on faith journeys together, but of course this is a long, slow journey. The church is very much behind what we are doing, though, and we have great support.

I'd definitely like to increase the group frequency. The demand is there, and I'm confident that I can 'give away' some of the organisational responsibilities.[4]

Schools

Churches have to work creatively to support the faith development of their children and young people. Rural children and young people are brought together for their education, so schools are an obvious place to focus work for these age groups. A number of initiatives have developed in recent years that follow this approach with some success. The drawback is that village churches may not see the fruit of the work in their congregations.

Where the majority of pupils live locally, there is the opportunity to run a Christian-based after-school club. If most of the pupils have to travel some distance to attend the school(s) in your area, it may be better to offer a lunchtime club.

Open the Book

Another scheme that has met with considerable success is Open the Book. This scheme started in Bedford in 1999 and now operates in some 1500 schools across the country. A small team of volunteers (which can be as small as two people) arranges with a primary school to visit weekly to provide a 10- to 15-minute Bible-based assembly. They follow a prepared outline, which links with National Curriculum goals.[5] Each team develops its own way of sharing the story, which can be as simple as reading it while sitting in a rocking chair, or a more exuberant version that involves acting it out with props and costumes and lots of pupil participation. Most schools are delighted to have a weekly assembly delivered for them, and churches feel that they are sharing Bible stories in a simple but effective way. The relationships built in this way often lead to schools visiting local churches as part of their Religious Education programme.

Revd Jane Willis, vicar of the Chittleleigh churches in North Devon, is delighted to have two teams of volunteers visiting the primary schools in the area. They use the standard Open the Book material but have developed a range of inventive props to illustrate the stories they share. The volunteers and children value the fun approach and the relationships they have built over the years. The Open the Book volunteers scripted and led the Christmas crib service so that visiting children would recognise the same people who regularly go into their school.

Prayer Spaces in Schools

A number of churches, often working in ecumenical partnership, offer to organise prayer spaces in their local school.

Prayer Spaces in Schools enable children and young people to explore faith and spirituality from a broadly Christian perspective in a safe, creative and interactive way. A range of flexible resources can be adapted to work for participants aged five to 18, bringing an experiential dimension to a variety of subject areas and to pastoral aspects of school life.[6]

Prayer spaces can involve a huge amount of work for a few individuals, but, if those people love being creative as they pray, they will surely be blessed by this approach.

The first step is to approach the school to offer to organise a prayer space and to explain what it would involve. If the school is interested, negotiations take place to find a date and suitable space in the school, and to decide which year groups will be invited. In small rural schools, it is likely that all pupils from Reception to Year 6 will have an opportunity to visit the prayer space during curriculum time. In larger schools, the invitation to visit may be limited to a single year group or Key Stage. Some primary schools like to offer a prayer space to Year 6 pupils after their SATS, as part of their period of transition to secondary school; well-planned prayer activities can allow the pupils to address their concerns about moving up to a bigger school. Additional access may also be offered at break or lunchtime.

Apart from creating the prayer space and providing all the materials, volunteers are present in the room to help children use the different activities and to replenish materials as required. The volunteers do not have to be experienced in working with children or young people, although they must have Disclosure and Barring Service clearance. It is important that volunteers are calm and sensitive to the possibilities of the occasion. The Prayer Spaces in Schools website provides a useful step-by-step guide that gives all the information required. This approach works well in both primary and secondary schools.

Flore prayer space
Rachel Roxburgh, a teacher and parent, organised a prayer space in Flore Primary School, Northamptonshire.

I led an assembly alongside our rector to introduce the prayer space on the Friday before it opened. All 111 children in the school came to the prayer space in small groups of four to six, with every class participating on a different day. Each group had 45 minutes in the space and were encouraged to try all ten activities individually, as well as having an introductory and closing session around the globe, as a group.

The ten prayer activities were:

- The worry box (posting our worries to God)
- God's heart (writing names of people/animals/things we love, as God loves us)
- Sorry sand (asking for forgiveness, then rubbing out our regrets)
- God's hand (writing our names on it, to show we are all part of God's family)
- Praying for the world (paper chain prayers around the globe, focusing on recent global events)
- Our prayer wall (for general prayers)
- Thinking of homeless children (experiencing climbing into a box and sleeping bag, looking at photos of homeless children and writing prayers for them on the box)
- Fizzy forgiveness (dropping an effervescent vitamin tablet into a small tub of water and experiencing the changes to the look, smell and sound of the water; this symbolised letting go and forgiving others, while recognising any changes inside ourselves as a result of forgiveness)
- Thank-you board (prayers of thanks for good things in our lives)
- 'Be still' prayer tent (a reflective atmosphere with gentle acoustic worship music, Bible verses, beanbags and soft lighting)

We found that nearly all the children wanted to do every activity and some did several more than once. Their responses were astonishingly profound, thoughtful and heartfelt, with some children becoming quite emotional about things they had said and written. All responded calmly, sensibly and genuinely to the prayer activities, producing incredibly touching feedback.

All staff members were really positive about the effect the prayer space was having on the children, as well as about the space itself. Personally, I felt a deep sense of peace and purpose during the week. Parents came in to view the project during the last couple of afternoons. The pupils were asked to feed back on the experience and their comments included:

'We enjoyed the little "Be still" corner. Thank you for making the activities such fun.'

· 'Thank you for organising the prayer space; it was very inspiring and emotional.'

'It got rid of the bad feelings and made room for the good feelings' (referring to the 'Fizzy forgiveness' activity).

The small size of the groups visiting the Flore prayer space reflects the dimensions of the room in which it was set up. Often, prayer spaces can accommodate 15 or more children at a time, but they don't have to be so large if space is limited.

Buildings

Some rural children and young people may have a particular attachment to a church or chapel in their village. They are more likely to attend an occasional office, such as a baptism or funeral, than their urban counterparts, and more likely to know neighbours who attend on Sundays. The church or chapel is often the largest building in the village and may offer the only meeting space. Rural churches are more often left open during the day and this provides opportunities for engaging with young people and children as well as adults.

In the church at Whissendine in Rutland, there is a second-hand bookstall/lending library. Books for children and young people are free to borrow. This is an idea that could easily be developed into a weekly drop-in session with drinks available and somewhere to 'hang out'. A more radical plan might be to redevelop the interior of the building to provide a badminton court or a climbing wall, while retaining the flexibility required for worship. The Tubestation at Polzeath, Cornwall, is an early example of a church that was redeveloped to provide skateboarding facilities and a café to meet the needs of young people. The building also provides a valuable community space for meetings. Worship, prayer and faith development underpin everything that happens at the Tubestation.[7]

Many rural churches lack running water but this need not be a bar to offering activities for children. The church at Pytchley, Northamptonshire, hires a portable lavatory to be sited discreetly in the churchyard, so that it can run a holiday club week each summer in its own building.

The Wesley Playhouse

Birstall is a large village, six miles from Leeds. Caroline Holt, a church steward, visited a commercial indoor playpark and thought it would be good if a church developed a similar attraction, but with Christian values. The Wesley Playhouse, in Howden Clough Methodist Church, Birstall,[8] now offers 3000 square feet of play area and a well-used café. The investment was huge but a good number of baptisms have come from the families who use the facility. There is a purpose-designed chapel for Sunday worship and a monthly 'Playhouse Praise', intended for the families who use the play facilities. One of the big challenges is not to allow the Playhouse to become just a business, but to maintain its focus on outreach while ensuring that it can pay its way.

The churchyard

Some village churches have developed their churchyards in ways that are attractive to children and families. Eco-Congregation is a project of A Rocha, the environmental charity. A visit to their website[9] provides plenty of ideas to involve children, young people and adults in 'creation care'. A well-planned environmental project is a powerful way to build relationships and address issues of Christian stewardship. Many people, of all ages, may take their first steps towards joining a church by first getting involved in a green project in which they already have an interest.[10]

The church in Newton Bromswold, on the border of Northamptonshire and Bedfordshire, has won awards for its conservation work. Children are encouraged to explore the churchyard and to identify the many different kinds of wildlife to be discovered. This is an extension of the clear statement on the church's website that they are an inclusive church, providing services and activities for all ages and stages of life. This kind of project offers scope to involve children and young people in the actual conservation work.

Resource limitations

One of the difficulties faced by rural congregations is that of resources. Ministers are likely to have responsibility for several churches, and these churches may be some distance from each other, which means that the minister spends much time in travelling. Finances may be tight and worshippers scattered across a wide area. Adults, young people and children may have to commute some distance to work or school, so a village may feel empty during the day.

In rural areas, one of the answers to a lack of resources is working in partnership with other churches, across denominational boundaries and with other groups and organisations in the community and wider area.

There is also a clear need to identify the assets that the church building, congregation and community already have. For example, the church may be the only public meeting space left in a village, particularly if the school or pub has closed. The church can become the polling booth for elections and a meeting space for public sessions of the parish council. The building, with very little adaptation, can become a lending library and a drop-in space.

Church buildings can also host movie nights for families or young people. You only need a large screen, a digital projector and the means to play a DVD. The terms of the Church Video Licence do not permit an admission fee to be charged, but the sale of refreshments is permitted, as are donations.[11] An initiative such as this, though, is a good way of encouraging young people and families to come into the building, so free hospitality and a good welcome may be a better approach.

Another positive side to rural life is that there may be few competing activities. This means that attendance can be high at the events that churches do put on. Holiday clubs may provide much-needed company for lonely children when they are not at school, as well as valuable childcare for the benefit of parents. The Christian Partnership Council of Hutton Rudby, in North Yorkshire, operates a computer club for young people across the village, as well as a holiday club.

However, it must be recognised that people are often reluctant to travel out of their village to attend church anywhere else. Some groups of churches have tried offering a Sunday school in each of four churches in turn through the month. In practice, families tend to support the one in their own church and lack the motivation to travel on the other Sundays.

Youth workers

In north Cornwall, a partnership between a fresh expression and a Church of England benefice of several churches has raised money to employ a children's worker. The worker visits the primary schools in the area to take assemblies and lead after-school sports clubs, as well as helping with the development of a Messy Church and other church-based activities.

The success of such projects comes from one person having the vision and passion to drive the project, lead the initial negotiations and start finding supporters. This lead person will often line-manage the worker and continue to pursue funding for the post. As the saying goes, 'every project needs a parent'! However, it is vitally important that the lead person builds a team of people around them to help sustain enthusiasm, make use of a wide skill base and share responsibility.

One reason that such projects may falter, apart from financial support drying up, is that the various church congregations expect the employed worker to do all the work—and preferably in their own church building. In practice, while the worker may do some specific activities themselves, such as speaking in school assemblies, one of their key roles will be to find, enthuse, train and deploy volunteers to lead much of the work. When this is done well, with volunteers being helped to grow into leadership, different pieces of work are likely to continue after the paid worker has departed.

Working ecumenically

Ecumenical cooperation is a powerful witness in villages. By contrast, having two Messy Churches, for example, run in the same village but by different churches, is not the best way forward. In Yardley Hastings, Northamptonshire, there is a successful Messy Church run by the United Reformed Church and the Anglican Church in partnership, to the delight of the families. In Harrold, Bedfordshire, the Anglican vicar is also the minister for the United Reformed Church. Under her leadership, a joint holiday club has been developed for local children and families.

However, it takes much trust between the partnering churches and a generosity of spirit to overcome difficulties. It can be hard to see work with children and young people flourishing in one church when much of the funding and many of the volunteers come from another congregation. This may well happen when one church has more adaptable buildings, while another has a larger attendance and thus a bigger capacity to provide funding and people. God's kingdom is greater than our own territorial concerns, though. It is important, as Rowan Williams has said, to 'find out what God is doing—and join in'. If the Holy Spirit blesses one piece of work, let us pray for the generosity to thank God for it, without feeling aggrieved that it is not happening in our own building or community.

Some dioceses and denominational regions run intern schemes for young adults (usually) to explore ministry or gain training in youth work. These schemes are another way for a group of churches to get help with leading youth work. Because the internships are usually for a year, it may be possible to raise the finance required for this limited period while kick-starting or developing some youth work that will endure. Another way to provide youth work is to link with a much bigger organisation. For example, South West Youth Ministries (SWYM) provides training placements in a wide range of churches across Cornwall, Devon and Somerset. SWYM provides training for the apprentice, who, in turn, helps to develop youth or children's work in the sponsoring church. The host church provides the trainee with board and accommodation and modest expenses, as well as contributing towards the cost of training.[12]

The report *From Anecdote to Evidence*,[13] produced by the Church of England in 2014, indicates that making an effort to work with children and young people is usually fruitful. Churches with a higher ratio of children to adults are likely to be growing in attendance. Churches that offer worship services designed with children in mind are also likely to grow. Rural churches need to think carefully about these findings, starting by finding out how many children and young people are present in their communities and asking parents and the children themselves what they might like the church to do. Some of the ideas in this chapter may be the place to start building new relationships with children, families and young people.

Notes

1 www.table-talk.org
2 www.freshexpressions.org.uk/stories/playandpraise
3 www.wholetthedadsout.org.uk
4 www.germinate.net/go/dads
5 Available from www.openthebook.net
6 www.prayerspacesinschools.com
7 www.freshexpressions.org.uk/stories/tubestation
8 www.freshexpressions.org.uk/stories/playhouse
9 http://ew.ecocongregation.org
10 See also www.caringforgodsacre.org.uk
11 Full details can be found at: http://churches.ccli.co.uk/licences/cvl
12 Full details can be found at www.swym.org.uk
13 www.churchgrowthresearch.org.uk/UserFiles/File/Reports/FromAnecdoteToEvidence1.0.pdf

Developing Messy Church

Simon Martin

A member of a rural congregations writes:

It's Messy Church in the Village Hall. As the clock approaches 4.00 on a Sunday afternoon, we're almost ready to go. Eight tables are laid out with activities related to the theme of 'invisible God': paper planes, magnetic fishing, bread making, bubble painting and kite making. When it comes to the celebration in an hour, we'll talk about the forces we can't see but can experience: wind, gravity, fermentation, magnetism. Then we'll connect this idea to a dramatic telling of the Pentecost story and finish with a song and a prayer, before we turn to the meal together. Around the tables, helpers in their Messy Church T-shirts make final preparations. Team members in the kitchen put the pizza in the oven and the choc ices in the freezer. Some of the team have little connection with the more traditional local congregation. The welcome desk is ready, with the sign-up form, name labels and a hand-out. Behind the desk is a baby-and-parent area. Every child in the village school has had a flyer to take to their parents and it's been round the village eNews. We pray together and (with a note of relief!) watch the first few groups turn towards the hall.

There is a large and growing number of Messy Churches across the country. By mid-2015 there were just under 3000 registered, with plenty more starting. Within the UK, Messy Churches can be found from Shetland to the southernmost tip of Cornwall, and from Northern Ireland via Cardigan Bay to the Norfolk coast. There is good reason to believe that well over a quarter of them are in rural locations.

The Messy Church approach catches the imagination of ministers and congregations alike in churches of all denominations and in a wide range of locations. It involves and empowers a large number of people who would otherwise be unlikely to engage in direct mission. Messy Church relies on teamwork. The operation of a team—its creation, development and support—is a vital element of Messy Church. It draws into the wider orbit of the community of Christ substantial numbers of non-churchgoers—and not just children but their parents and extended families too. In rural situations, starting a Messy Church has helped to encourage small congregations to work together, sometimes across denominational boundaries. Other rural churches have benefited from using the increasing range of resources and approaches to work with children, young people and all ages.

Some see Messy Church as a subsection of the broader Fresh Expressions movement, and there is no doubt that there are distinct similarities in ethos and approach. However (especially within the rural context), Messy Church as a movement for mission has strong links to pre-existing churches and congregations that many fresh expressions do not share. Messy Church represents a mixed economy approach, incorporating strengths from both traditional and innovative ways of doing and being church.

Messy Church is no panacea; it is not an instant solution for successful mission in rural communities. But it is something new, and it holds real potential for small churches in small communities, many of which will be rural.

Huge hearts, small congregations: case study

Bar Nash-Williams is Newcastle Diocesan Development Officer for Youth Work in West Northumberland, based at the United Benefice of Stamfordham with Matfen. She writes as the leader of a newly launched Messy Church.

It starts with the heart

All the good plans and keen participation come to nothing if you don't start with the heart. It's your heart that says, 'It's worth it for just one child.' It's the heart that says, 'We do what we can, and trust to God for the rest.' When you start with that attitude, a tiny church can do good things with limited resources.

We've done six Messy Church sessions now, three in Matfen and three in the slightly larger village in our benefice. The biggest number we've welcomed is around 45 (children and adults) and the smallest is eleven. When we only have a small number, we and they still enjoy it, and the church grows in confidence each time.

Matfen church is small and full of ancient pews, across which trestle tables sit nicely, even though it's hard for our less agile leaders to crawl under them. It has no loo, no kitchen and no water. For a while, recently, it had no floor and lots of tripping hazards. It still has crumbling plaster and no carpet. An ideal place to try a really Messy Church—messy science, with exploding pop bottles, squishing eggs, vinegar and bicarb volcanoes—you know the sort of thing.

We have a small congregation, usually between ten and 15 people, mostly grandparent age. Each member of the usual congregation has gifts and abilities, and each child or adult who comes to Messy Church is a valued member of the village community, loved by God and worth the church's time and attention. It's a small village, with a village hall that kindly offers us loos and space for food and games, especially if it's too cold to eat and play outdoors.

'Shy bairns get nowt'

We always try to involve a good proportion of the usual congregation. We usually have the vicar, another member of the shared ministry team, and one or two others at the planning meeting, although the actual members of the team vary each time. Then, when we ask for help, we try to keep it simple and specific.

We don't just say, 'Please come and help at the next Messy Church.' People don't think they're good with children, or that they can do craft, or whatever. So we are much more specific, and limited, in our requests. We might say:

- Who can help with the candle experiment and guide our young teen helper?
- We need a tray of coconut pyramids: who likes baking?
- We need someone to take photos: who is good with a camera?

As they say up here, 'Shy bairns get nowt.' We ask people who don't come to church to share a skill or an interest we've heard they have, and we ask the handful of teens we know in the village if they will support the adults. We are very careful to make sure no one feels guilty if they can't help. If we can't get enough helpers for each activity, we do one less than we'd planned.

The ringing round or visiting to ask is useful contact in itself, and leads to some valuable conversations, even pastoral encounters.

Feel the fear and do it anyway

Make no mistake, it all still feels precarious, fragile, hand-to-mouth and last-minute. It all seems likely to collapse just before it happens each time. But it hasn't yet. We've always had some families joining us, and we're beginning to get to know them. We pray for the grace to persevere until we've really built up the kinds of relationships and trust that let people share at a deeper level.

Messy Church DNA?

It is becoming increasingly common to describe certain sorts of organisations or movements in terms of their 'DNA'. Taking a cue from the realms of genetics and heredity, an organisation's DNA is shorthand for its underlying blueprint, evident in the way the organisation operates and what it produces.

An organism's DNA contains all the information required for the full development of every cell in a viable adult individual, but different cells draw on different parts of this blueprint, resulting in a vast range of different cells, organs and other structures. They are distinct yet connected by, and reflecting, the same underlying DNA. Likewise, individual Messy Churches have developed from the same underlying principles, approach and ethos. Each one is different, however, moulded by the unique context in which it has grown and developed, the needs of the communities it serves, and the unique set of skills and experiences of the team members.[1]

What is the DNA of Messy Church?

From the start, Messy Church has emphasised a fivefold set of underlying values: creative, hospitable, all-age, Christ-centred and celebratory (worshipping). This forms the backbone of the values and approach that all Messy Churches are encouraged to adopt.

- **Hospitable:** food as a central element in a consciously missional approach.
- **Creative:** crafts, activity and, above all, hands-on involvement.
- **Celebratory:** worship and community together.
- **All-age:** relevant and transformational for whole families.

- **Christ-centred:** honouring Christ and communicating his good news.

However, I would like to add a sixth element to these five—'incarnational', showing Christ in relationships, attitudes and behaviour.

This is not in any way a specifically rural element of Messy Church, but I believe it is one that is especially prominent for Messy Churches that operate in small (and, thus, quite often rural) communities. These are places where people often know their neighbours rather well, where their attitudes and behaviour are often closely observed, and where changes in the activities and habits of individuals or households are quickly noticed. The lives of Messy Church team members will be scrutinised inside and outside the church and will be the clearest evidence that Messy Church participants will present of a developing relationship with Christ.

In addition, rural Messy Churches tend to draw on a larger pool of non-churchgoing helpers and even core team members. These people will be planning, working, laughing, crying and even praying alongside the helpers and team members who are already Christians. For them, it can be almost an apprenticeship in the Christian faith, shadowing those who already demonstrate their own living faith.

Behind all this lie both flexibility and risk, which are significant aspects of the Messy Church ethos. The Bible Reading Fellowship (BRF), of which Messy Church is a ministry, has deliberately chosen a hands-off, non-controlling approach, in the hope 'that this will give God space to grow his church in the way he wants to, and that it will give everyone encouragement to experiment and innovate'.[2] There is no guarantee that those starting a Messy Church will faithfully incorporate all the values that the movement enshrines. Anybody can obtain and use the material, and any group can adopt as much or as little of the Messy Church approach as they like and still call themselves Messy Church. (Conversely, there are groups that have fully adopted the Messy Church ethos and approach but, for a variety of reasons, have chosen not to call themselves Messy Church.)

This flexibility has helped to generate the great diversity of types of Messy Church, but there are significant potential difficulties. Firstly, Messy Church might be seen simply as a method to be copied (welcome, craft activity, worship, food) but without taking on board and exhibiting the ethos and values. Secondly, key elements of Messy Church values might be misunderstood or abandoned—for example, suggesting that it is for children only, not for everyone.

One small rural church with a usual congregation of maybe a dozen, most of whom were past retirement age, had been helping to run a Messy Church for six months. It had drawn in quite a few families with children from the local community, but the benefit had not all been for the families and children coming into the Messy Church.

The church's minister reflects:

Several of the congregation live on their own and, although they wouldn't complain, are beginning to experience a certain amount of isolation and even loneliness, accompanied by decreased mobility that has come with advancing age. Most have found something of a new lease of life by getting involved with Messy Church and the local families. They thoroughly enjoy helping, preparing and serving food and, most of all, chatting with the children and their parents, praying for them and taking an interest in their lives outside Messy Church. In two cases, 'honorary grannies' seem to have been inaugurated!

In a small way, Messy Church has helped to provide a surrogate family for these older people, especially for those whose own families live much further away. In addition, the children are introduced to an older generation with whom they would otherwise have little contact.

What Messy Church isn't!

There are genuine misconceptions about Messy Church, many of them reflecting various actual experiences.[3]

- It isn't just for children. It's much easier to aim a Messy Church at one particular age group, but what does this say about God? If your Messy Church's teaching, crafts and food are all aimed at the under-elevens, what message are the children and adults picking up? That church is only relevant, fun, meaningful or interested in you until you're twelve? No, Messy Church needs to be constantly creative in its thinking about how to involve very different people: young and old, families and single people, male and female, reflective and practical, poor and rich. It isn't called 'church' for nothing.
- It isn't a children's club. The whole of Messy Church is about worshipping God, having fellowship, exploring faith. It welcomes everyone, involves everyone, values everyone, and is always there for the outsider. It's a church. There are some groups calling themselves Messy Churches where the majority of the parents sit around the sides while their children are 'occupied' with the activities or 'going off' for the worship. This is a mistake; among other things, it robs both adults and children of a shared experience.
- It isn't a way of getting people to come to 'real church'. It

won't do this, except in a few rare cases. If people wanted to come to traditional church, they would be coming by now. Messy Church is interdependent with traditional church, but will usually operate as a separate congregation. As the story below from the West Midlands shows (see pages 174–175), church leaders need to recognise this early on. There are plenty of Messy Churches that provide church for many people who have never attended traditional church services. In recognition of this, Messy Churches (with the support of regional and national church leaders) are developing ways of celebrating the breadth of church life: conversion, Eucharist, baptism, confirmation and weddings, to say nothing of the demanding pilgrimage of daily discipleship and maturing in faith.

- It isn't just for churchgoers and their families. Anyone can get involved in leading and running a Messy Church, how ever old or young they are, and this gives an opportunity to draw in others who aren't already involved in the church. One of the delights of many people's experience of a Messy Church is welcoming non-churchgoers on to the wider leadership team, as was illustrated in the earlier story from Northumberland (see page 161). Asking people to share their interests, skills and views, and sharing responsibilities in return, helps greatly in creating and sustaining a worshipping community. An earlier generation sometimes talked of 'gossiping the gospel'—sharing it in an informal, over-the-back-fence manner. Informality and personal interaction are part of the Messy Church ethos, and remain a successful way of drawing people to Christ.

- It isn't only for 'traditional families'. All are welcome— single parents, nuclear families, separated, single, widowed, childless, divorced and so on. The only basic relationship requirement is that any children who come are expected to be accompanied by an adult, although, even here, a certain flexibility is acceptable, with younger children sometimes accompanied by teenage siblings. Church is inclusive, not exclusive. However, sadly, there are groups where adults arriving without children have not been welcomed or encouraged to take part in some of the elements of the time together (for example, being asked, 'You won't want to do the crafts, will you?').

- It isn't a quick fix. Growing disciples takes time. Messy Church has only been running for a few years anywhere. It usually only meets once a month, and not everyone is likely to come to each meeting. Hence, continuity can be an issue, and growth will probably be slow—in numbers, in levels of commitment, and in the degree of spiritual awareness and faith development. Messy Church is not a 'magic bullet' to solve all of a church's evangelism, mission or discipleship issues, although it is an innovative, exciting and genuinely attractive approach. If congregation members were not actively seeking ways to engage in appropriate mission and evangelism before they thought of starting Messy Church, the same barriers are likely to continue to operate. Starting and running a Messy Church doesn't absolve a church from its ongoing, general responsibility for bearing witness, encouragement, nurture, community engagement and sacrificial service.

- It isn't an easy option. It takes prayer, time, money, commitment and energy from the whole church and the leadership team. Somebody once described starting a Messy Church in terms of the warnings in the preface to the marriage service in The Book of Common Prayer: 'not to be entered into unadvisedly or lightly, but reverently, deliberately, and in accordance with the purposes for which it was instituted by God'!

- It isn't a one-way relationship or drain on resources. Yes, it will take time, effort, money and gifted people to run it, but it will give back in return a group of people who are fired up for mission, empowered by using their God-given gifts. It will spark off ideas and inspiration about what church is all about and will renew vision. It will grow goodwill in the community towards the church, and most importantly, provide the opportunity to do effective mission in your own community.

Messy Church is not just a fun social activity, but an opportunity for people to discover Jesus. There are (or should be) lots of interesting, exciting and fun components in the average Messy Church gathering, not least because this is a real part of learning about Jesus, developing relationships with others and creating community. But these elements don't constitute the fundamental purpose of gathering families and others together for two hours once a month: rather, the gathering is to help them discover Jesus, develop a living Christian faith and grow in the likeness of Christ. Messy Church is, at its crudest, a tool to enable this growth to happen.

It is not just about getting the mechanics right, whether of the regular gatherings, the team of helpers or the core team. Rather, it is about the quality of the faith, hope and love that are demonstrated by the Christians within the Messy Church. The incarnational element will be evident through the lives, behaviour, attitudes, conversations and relationships of the Christians involved in each Messy Church.

In the final analysis, as one rural Messy Church leader says:

Messy Church isn't an end in itself; it's a means to all kinds of growth. The value isn't just in getting new people to come and feel welcome and at home in the church building; it's the interaction between all who plan, provide, lead and encounter that builds us up as a congregation. It's the Spirit at work among you that will stay with every soul. If we can help people to notice where God is among us, then Messy Church won't be just a passing fad but a life-changing resource.

The practicalities of Messy Church in rural churches

The team

Messy Church does require a team. It can't be done if one person takes it on alone. The problem is often that there are too few people to make up a team, or that people think of themselves as being too old or infirm. This presents an immediate opportunity to work with others in the wider community, such as parents from school or toddler groups, the non-worshipping spouses of church members, or teenagers doing their Duke of Edinburgh Award. An alternative and valuable approach is to develop a partnership with other churches in the area, either ecumenically or within the same denomination. The challenge of running a Messy Church can also help to revitalise your existing congregation, providing a mission-focused, outward-looking but non-threatening task to achieve together.

Older people, with their great life experience and serenity, can make excellent team leaders. Messy Church requires all sorts of jobs to be done; it's not just furniture shifters who are needed, but a prayer support team, craft helpers, cooks, welcomers, people to chat to the participants, and leaders for the celebration. There is a role for everyone who is prepared to join in: age and infirmity are no object or excuse.

One of the blessings of many Messy Church teams is that they bring together people at all stages in their journeys of faith. Another is that the team can be an effective vehicle for growing disciples and becoming a small community as they meet, eat, pray and plan together.

The building

Many rural Messy Churches will have to decide between holding Messy Church in the church building, with all its inconveniences, and holding it in a building that has all the facilities needed but might suggest a disassociation with church. The presence or absence of toilets in the church building may be the sole deciding factor. It is impossible, in this day and age, to invite families with children to an event without making a toilet available. The presence or absence of catering facilities is also a crucial factor, since eating together should form a significant part of all Messy Church sessions.

One Messy Church leader from Warwickshire explains:

We took the decision to have our meetings in church. We had a major reordering project a couple of years ago, so we now have a decent kitchen, toilets, heating and meeting rooms, and the flexibility to create large areas of space. The church is at the centre of the village and I want families to feel comfortable coming into the building and to associate it with having fun.

Clergy involvement

Some Messy Churches are lay led, with the assistance of a minister. In a number of rural examples, the local minister has deliberately maintained a policy of non-involvement, while providing background support. As one Methodist minister indicates, 'I see my place as encouraging and enabling my chapel congregations to get fully involved in planning and running the Messy Church. To start with, it was hard going... but new people are being drawn in directly, without me being involved at all.'

Publicity

It may well be an advantage to be in a village, where the word-of-mouth grapevine is much more effective than in a large town, but this method should not be relied on as the sole means of communication. In a large circuit or benefice, children may attend several different primary or secondary schools, while their families relate to one or more market towns and work in a great many different places. Publicity and communication are therefore essential, by every means possible. Many churches already have good relationships with schools or uniformed organisations, and putting a note into a book-bag at school (with permission) is usually well worth the effort. As the above-mentioned Warwickshire Messy Church leader says, 'It is invaluable to have good relationships with the local primary school and Scout group. They are more than happy to publicise our events.'

Old-fashioned noticeboards and church or community newsletters are just as important as social media and websites, particularly if you want to ensure that Messy Church really is for all ages. Listing the actual planned activities can be more effective in generating interest than something more generic. Make use of the logo as much as possible, as it is attractive and easy to identify. It can be used in newsletter articles and on posters in the pub, village shop (if you have one) and noticeboards outside the church and through the community. Many have found that a banner or A-frame, with a large 'Messy Church Today' sign, is a good way of reminding people who are passing the church. You can also start an email or text list that people opt into, so that they can be reminded when it is taking place. A Facebook group is also a good idea, but remember to get signed permission from parents or guardians to publish any pictures of children.

'Ownership' of the local church

Even in a dormitory village, there may be more of a latent sense of ownership of the local church building than there is in an urban area. This may mean that there is more goodwill towards the church simply as a symbol of the community, and a desire for what it does to work well. Messy Church is fun, so families may be more likely to come and support it, for the sake of the community, than in a town or suburb. This could be the case, especially, if there are few local groups or activities that involve children—but it then remains important that Messy Church is not mistakenly seen as a children's club.

Thinking outside the box

Messy Church requires lots of resources and helpers, and in rural, small or isolated communities it can be a challenge to bring everything together. However, with a little imaginative thinking, a few of the problems can be solved.

* One team can prepare the same Messy Church session to deliver at several different churches across an area.
* Work together: several churches or communities can run a single Messy Church.
* Rearrange pews to make better space, putting tabletops on the backs of pews or even going outside when the weather permits.

- Hire a portable loo if the venue has no toilet facilities available.
- Ask the Women's Institute or Mothers' Union to help with the food.
- BRF produces a lot of easy-to-use resources to support Messy Church, but you can also be creative, especially in relation to what is happening in your local community.
- Make use of seasonal or local festivals, such as harvest or a carnival, and celebrate them with Messy activities.
- To encourage more people to come, get Messy Church involved in a wide range of community activities, such as pond clearing, ditch tidying and litter picking, and follow up with a picnic or barbeque.
- Provide hospitality and Messy activities for families during fun runs or cycle rides.
- Have a stall at a local show or community fête and do a pop-up Messy Church.

Renita Boyle describes the approach of a Messy Church in rural Galloway:

Our Messy Church in Wigtown is very community-orientated. We've entered a NativiTree [a Christmas tree decorated to tell the story of the nativity] into a local display of Christmas trees; decorated our own aprons and entered two teams into the community pancake flipping relay; made shadow and matchbox puppets and performed the story of Jonah; and had a Messy Bramble Ramble, collecting blackberries (with food, stories, songs and crafts) and making Messy bramble jelly. In future, we hope to have a seaside expedition to explore sea-themed Bible stories, tell the story of Zacchaeus under the old yew tree in our churchyard, and run a half-day community workshop to make gingerbread nativity scenes.

Better together?

Many groups of rural churches are large in number, covering many small communities and a large geographical area. Individually these congregations would not be able to do Messy Church, but (to emphasise a point already made) by working together and doing things jointly, it would be possible.

Bright ideas and stimuli

Churchwardens from various parishes in rural Worcestershire were talking about starting a Messy Church. 'It looks like a good idea.' 'But it's too much for any of our parishes individually.' 'Yes, we're all so small.' Finally came the suggestion, 'Maybe we should do it together?'

A group from a Methodist chapel in the north-east of England talked about how they were getting different denominations together to start 'something new' with children and families 'in our dale'. They are now part of an ecumenical Messy Church seeing about 120 people coming each time, including at least 70 children, despite the fact that the original group members are few and elderly.

A Messy Church Regional Coordinator from south-west England talks of 'a team from several village churches who prepare a Messy Church and then travel to perhaps three villages to present it, have a rest for a few weeks and then begin the cycle again'. This model is now being tried in several rural Anglican deaneries.

In a West Midlands Anglican benefice, the vicar reflects:

We have two Messy Churches operating in our benefice; the one held in three small villages has been running for over a year. We meet in the village

174

halls as none of the churches have any water, only poor heating and no church hall. All are very traditional churches, with most of the congregations ageing. We started by challenging one congregation about what they would do to fulfil their baptism service promise to support the children that were being baptised. The PCC there agreed to drop a poorly attended family service and start Messy Church. A second church, and then a third, joined in.

We now have contact with many different families in the villages who would never have come to the normal church service (42 at the first meeting, typically 15–30 each month). The original PCC is fully behind the project and the older members of each congregation sort out the food when it is in their own village hall, alternating every three months.

I believe this is the future for these churches. Current congregations are elderly and, within 10–15 years, will be unlikely to have the energy to run church, even if they are still around. My hope is that we build on and develop Messy Church and disciple the parents as well as the children. I see this happening through engaging them in practical action rather than heavy teaching. For example, the Messy Church mums from the second village, none of whom are regular churchgoers, organised the harvest supper this year. This was the first time it had been run for years and they raised over £700 for a local hospice and famine relief in Africa.

I don't believe that Messy Church families will ever graduate into going to our traditional churches, but I hope that, through being engaged in action and developing new ideas as their children grow, they will replace the older churches as these congregations dwindle.

How to work together

Lucy Moore (founder of Messy Church) writes, in the introduction to a resource on running ecumenical Messy Church, that things may be better done together.

I am thrilled by the number of ecumenical or interdenominational Messy Churches starting up. To be honest, I'm thrilled when churches of the same denomination find the grace to work together and offer a joint Messy Church! Not just because we are the body of Christ, and different churches are like different body parts complementing each other, but also because of the Messy testimony it shouts out to the local community.[4]

Groups who have started an ecumenical or joint Messy Church have shared some of their most significant conclusions and advice.

- One person or church needs a clear vision of working together, which is then shared with the wider group.
- Get the leaders from each church on board at an early stage, as they may be nervous.
- Be ready to persist, as it will take time.
- Avoid giving leadership away to someone who may not be good at teamwork.
- You will need people from each church who have a vision for Messy Church and can work together to inspire their own congregation members.
- Once people have tasted Messy Church for themselves (for example, visiting a pre-existing group), it is easier for them to see how it might work in their situation.
- Allow at least six months of planning and preparation before you start.
- Designate a single organised person to head up the craft and activity team each month.
- Find a good cook, who is willing to help run a kitchen team.
- Make sure the whole team communicates what is going on.

- Make praying together a priority from the very first stages of planning, if for no other reason than it is much harder to have fights and arguments with people who you are praying for and with regularly.
- Working together takes a lot of effort, even more than running Messy Church for a single church or location, but is definitely worth it.
- Weigh up carefully the pros and cons of having Messy Church in the same place each time or moving from one church/community to another, perhaps in rotation. There is no single right answer. One leader says, 'In the autumn and winter we stay in one place, but in the spring and summer we move from village to village.'

After all this, if you feel encouraged to start a Messy Church in your rural location, there is plenty more help available. Besides the marvellous range of material from the Messy Church website (see www.messychurch.org.uk), there is a comprehensive series of resources on Messy Church in rural areas available from The Arthur Rank Centre:

- How best to use Messy Church in rural areas: www.germinate.net/go/ruralmc
- Rural Messy Church case studies: www.germinate.net/go/ruralmcexamples
- Messy discipleship (with a rural flavour): www.germinate.net/go/messydiscipleship

Notes

1 For a fuller discussion, see George Lings, 'What is the DNA of Messy Church?' in George Lings (ed.), *Messy Church Theology: Exploring the significance of Messy Church for the wider church* (Messy Church, 2013), pp. 154–173

2 www.messychurch.org.uk/what-messy-church-and-isnt

3 These points are an extended discussion of the material that can be found on www.messychurch.org.uk/what-messy-church-and-isnt

4 Lucy Moore and Jane Leadbetter, 'Ecumenical Messy Church', p. 2: http://ctbi.org.uk/wp-content/uploads/2014/11/Ecumenical-Messy-Church-report.pdf

Church buildings: serving the community and ministry to visitors

Becky Payne

Our church buildings need to offer a SPACE for God, a PLACE for people and a BASE for mission.[1]

The relationship between a congregation and its building can be both positive and negative. The care of a building is not the primary reason why people join a church, yet congregations find themselves responsible for a place that (they may feel) drains their resources and prevents them from doing certain things, and a place over which other organisations have a say. Many of our churches are under-utilised and, for many congregations, the burden of looking after historic buildings falls on a small group of volunteers.

Many outside the church view our buildings, often the oldest and most prominent in the area, as powerful symbols of stability. The building is seen as a keeper of community stories and traditions, and as providing a sense of the spiritual. Increasingly, congregations are rediscovering the role that church buildings can play in their mission, working with others in their communities to develop new uses, recreating them as assets for the whole community. Buildings are then used for up to seven days a week rather than one in seven. This can often provide a more secure future for the building and reconnect the church with the wider community.

The key is to start with mission. What is God calling you to do? Decide what it is you want to achieve and then look at how your resources—building, people and finances—can help you achieve your objectives. A building project on its own is not going to build a congregation, provide a service to the wider community or help you engage with your wider community.

Ministry to visitors

The Churches Visitor and Tourism Association says, 'We believe that church buildings are at the forefront of the Church's mission. Our buildings proclaim—in wood, stone, glass and metal—that "God is in the midst" of every community.'[2]

Tens of millions of people visit our cathedrals and churches every year. Keeping the building open and extending a welcome is the simplest way for the church to be a living presence for community and visitors alike. Church buildings belong to the whole community, so, to keep them closed to all but a few, on restricted occasions, gives the message that they belong only to the chosen few. An open church is a simple act of hospitality to everyone, whether worshippers, pilgrims or tourists.

There are many reasons why people visit churches.

- Church buildings bear witness to the Christian faith and offer a celebration of the presence of God in a community. An open church speaks of a welcoming Christian community and a welcoming God.
- An open church offers a sacred space at the heart of every community where local people and tourists can come and meet with God and find a place for quiet contemplation.
- Churches are treasure houses of history, from which people of all ages can learn about architecture, history,

craftsmanship and ancestry. Their stunningly beautiful interiors provide inspiration and succour to those leading busy, perhaps stressful lives.

- Churches are key keepers of community heritage, traditions and stories.
- Other faith groups and people from ethnic minority backgrounds have a genuine interest in finding out more about churches. Open churches can contribute to inter-faith understanding.

The many benefits of opening your doors include:

- opportunities to share faith and reach new audiences
- helping people to see that it is a living space
- the fact that public access is often a requirement of funders such as the Heritage Lottery Fund or other charities

When opening your church for visitors (tourists or pilgrims), the vision for hospitality should form part of all other policies and initiatives and inform all future plans, including developments to the building. Consider setting up an 'Open Church' group, which can develop the vision and work through the practical implications. Everyone in your church should be part of the discussion and should understand the implications of opening and what it means to be welcoming.

Barriers

Many rural churches are already open regularly, but for others this can be a challenge. Fears about theft, antisocial behaviour and personal safety are the three main reasons why churches are not open. These are genuine concerns. If you open and leave the building unattended, items may be taken. You may also be in an area where there are particular social problems, raising issues of personal safety and property damage. There may be a subconscious fear that people will come in who do not respect the building or the Christian faith.

However, without wanting to minimise the risks, many of these fears may only apply in very specific circumstances. It is sometimes assumed that insurance policies require churches to be locked but, in fact, an open church is less likely to suffer a theft. The advice of insurance company Ecclesiastical is that, provided the right precautions have been taken, 'where appropriate, churches are kept open because of the positive effect that has on security. The presence of legitimate visitors will help to deter those with a criminal intent.'[3]

Both Ecclesiastical and Methodist Insurance provide detailed advice on the practical measures you can put in place to mitigate risk. As long as you implement that advice, you will be covered for the cost of any theft or damage (and your premiums should not go up). It is often less expensive to replace items than to repair damage caused by break-ins.[4] There is also guidance available on good practice for personal safety.[5]

An opening strategy

When opening your church, the following questions need to be considered.

- What are the best times for the building to be open and what is realistically achievable?
- Will the building be unattended or will someone be present to welcome visitors and offer a discreet security presence?
- How does your building look to a stranger coming to it for the first time?

The small Methodist church of Cullen, Moray, in Scotland, has 'Open Door' every Wednesday between February and December, from 10.00 am to 11.30 am, for a 'cuppa and fellowship'.[6]

Providing a welcome

Visitors will appreciate it if they feel that they have been expected and that thought has been given to making them feel welcome. Many people are reluctant to open a closed church door because, for those who are not regular worshippers, a church building is unfamiliar and they do not feel immediately comfortable going inside. Some may come from a different cultural background or a different faith. Equally, many have come to expect church doors to be locked, so will not attempt to visit unless there are obvious signs of life. We need to break down those barriers. Many churches find that the number of visitors increases significantly when there is a welcoming 'Church open' sign outside. Your signage should be welcoming to all. A notice simply announcing that the church is 'open for prayer' may make some people feel that it is not for them.

Ideally, keep the door, or at least the outer door, physically open. You may want to redesign your entrance by installing glass doors, which allow people to see inside before they enter. They can be less daunting than a heavy traditional wooden door and allow the main doors to be open without letting cold air into the building.[7] You also need to think about physical access for wheelchair users, those who need to use a stick or crutches, and parents with pushchairs and toddlers.[8]

Communication

Telling people that the church building is open (as a new venture or an ongoing event) is essential. Put notices on noticeboards, in a community or parish magazine, and in local shops, pubs or other businesses. Opening times should also be clearly visible on the outside of the building. People increasingly expect to obtain information via their mobile phones and laptops, so use websites and social media or create a Wikipedia entry.

Other technologies allow potential visitors to look around your church in advance. For example, St Wulfram's Church in Grantham, Lincolnshire, has a 360° video tour on its website, which encourages visitors to come and see the real thing.[9]

Working with partners

Work in partnership with other nearby tourist attractions, pubs, restaurants and neighbouring churches, and promote each other by sharing leaflets. Join wider initiatives, such as Heritage Open Days and 'Ride and Stride'. Participate in a local arts festival by providing a venue, opening throughout the festival and offering tours and teas. These initiatives will provide publicity and other support. Make sure that your local or nearby Tourist Information Centres know that the church is open and have leaflets to encourage visitors.

There are now several long-standing church festivals, the best-known being the West Lindsey Churches Festival, now in its 18th year, which is sponsored by West Lindsey District Council, among others.[10]

The Diocese of Hereford is very clear about the importance of opening churches so that they stay at the heart of the community, and over 85 per cent of its churches are open daily. The diocese has produced practical guidance for churches on welcoming visitors[11] and has established two ecumenical tourism groups, one covering Hereford[12] and one covering Shropshire,[13] both of which have published county guides to all the open churches. The diocese is currently working with the Herefordshire Tourism and Food Strategy Group, through the Rural Hub and the Local Enterprise Partnership, to help write a strategy for tourism in Herefordshire, promoting church tourism as an economic driver.

In 2013, the Dioceses of Lichfield, Hereford and Worcester organised a Festival of Churches, with arts activities, family history, times of telling the Christian story, and refreshments. 237 churches participated, organising 291 individual events over one September weekend. In 2014, the festival took place over two weeks in September.[14]

What are you going to offer your visitors?

Saltaire United Reformed Church says to potential visitors, 'We don't want you to leave with the impression that you have merely seen a museum. The church is not simply wood and stone; the "Church" is the living community of people who regularly meet here to worship.'[15]

It is important to find the right balance between making people feel comfortable and providing them with information, while retaining a sense of awe by letting the building speak for itself. Be careful not to overfill the church with too many noticeboards and displays, which can create visual confusion. Exhibitions and displays are best placed close to the main entrance or in aisles or transepts.

There is a great deal that can be offered to visitors, but do you know who your current visitors are and why they are coming? A visitors' book will help. Here are some thoughts on other sorts of information you might want to offer.

- Provide materials for those who visit the church seeking a place of prayer. Use lighting to illuminate particular images, icons and statutes, or create a journey around the church with suggested prayers at particular points. People will expect to find a quiet space and perhaps somewhere to light a candle. Provide a book or slips of paper where people can write prayer requests.
- Tell visitors about the church as a place of worship and provide information about the Christian faith. Explain the function of items such as the altar, lectern and font. Consider producing a guide especially for children that combines these two elements.
- Introduce yourselves and the life of the church. Photographs of key people and recent activities can bring the work of your church to life. Provide information on any local community projects you are involved in and explain how new people can participate. List regular service times and make it clear that all are welcome.
- Create a small display about your church, telling the story of your building, its history, architecture and special features, any association with a famous person, family or historical events, and its connections with the history of the local area.
- You may want to offer a range of guides, such as a detailed guide for those with a special interest in architecture, and a more straightforward one describing the key features that every visitor should see and explaining why they are important for faith. Provide something interactive for

children, such as a quiz, dressing-up clothes or a treasure box.[16]

- Build an app that people can download on to their phones during their visit.
- Train volunteers so that they can offer guided tours on special open days.

Producing the right materials can require a lot of work. Some items may require investment, while others can be produced inexpensively. This is also an opportunity to involve the wider community and, perhaps, the local history society in producing the material. Always aim to provide high-quality materials that meet the needs of your visitors, to indicate that you value the presence of visitors. For example, the Friends of St Dunstan's, Cranbrook, in Kent, have created a downloadable resource for schools and other visitors.[17]

There is no single solution to the question of how and when to open your church doors. Every church will have to assess its own circumstances and determine the best way to be open safely. Many churches that decide to open more regularly find that the benefits are far beyond their expectations and outweigh the disadvantages. Welcoming people into your building can be the start of creating a whole new set of opportunities to re-engage with your local community.

Community use

Imagining new scenarios when stood in a familiar setting can be very challenging and can be hard to visualise. There is no formula for what will work in any given church; what is the perfect way forward for one parish and building could be totally inappropriate or ineffectual in another.[18]

Rural communities have lost many facilities, including post offices, banks, shops and pubs. Rural churches have an opportunity to evolve and adapt both outlook and buildings to meet these new circumstances by offering premises for vital community facilities.

This is not a new idea. Originally, the chancel was reserved for liturgy and worship and was the responsibility of the church, while the nave, owned and cared for by the local community, was used for a range of activities, including public meetings, theatrical events, elections and the education of children. Nowadays, it is accepted that churches can accommodate many uses, which need not be specifically ecclesiastical in purpose, provided that worship remains their primary purpose. Church Courts have held that the additional uses do not need to be ancillary to worship or pastoral in motivation.[19]

National and local government and public sector agencies are increasingly acknowledging the contribution of faith groups to social cohesion, education and regeneration. Recent research shows that faith groups have a special contribution to make, being deeply rooted in community life, able to reach out to the most vulnerable groups, and well placed to provide high-quality local public services.[20]

Across the UK, you will find examples of 'living' churches that are hosting a variety of activities, ranging from exhibitions and concerts to youth clubs and senior citizens' lunches. They also provide premises for school classes, community shops, farmers' markets, libraries, Citizens Advice, health services, community police, banks and post offices.

Community use will enable the church to continue as a place of worship while, at the same time, helping to meet a specific community need. Varying degrees of physical intervention may be required to adapt the church building; some activities may require very little, if any, adaptation, while others will involve considerable changes. Projects such as these help to build and strengthen relationships with the community and are more likely to succeed if a wider group of people shares responsibility for the adaptation and ongoing maintenance of the building. There may also be potential to help secure the future of the building by generating an income. These activities may be managed by the church, an outside organisation or a partnership between the two. There are many good examples of extended use of churches for community benefit; here are just a few.

- The parish church in Louth, Lincolnshire, hosts an access point for the local credit union.[21]
- St Margaret's Church, Wicken Bonhunt, in Essex, has been adapted and refurbished to provide a community space and place of worship.[22]
- St Michael and All Angels Church, Spencers Wood, in Oxfordshire, has set up a community café.[23]
- The new community shop in Buckland Brewer, North Devon, is in the Methodist church.[24]
- The United Reformed Church chapel in the Chalke Valley, Wiltshire, has been adapted to become a community hub, with a shop, post office, café and ecumenical church.[25]
- The Wold Valley Methodist Church, Weaverthorpe, in North Yorkshire, hosts an outreach post office.[26]

Meeting the practical challenges

Any project, even a small one with minimal changes to a building, will involve vision, hard work, determination and a team of people. There is no denying that making changes to almost any type of church building can be very complex. Additional sensitivity may well be needed, as many view churches as sacred places, and the building may be greatly loved by its community, even if people do not share the faith of those who worship there.

What are the important aspects of a successful project to bring a church into wider community use?

Developing your vision

Developing a mission statement (sometimes called a Mission Action Plan) for your place of worship is the first step. It should not only be part of a wider plan for mission in the community but should underpin any proposals to change or develop the building. It is important to be clear about why you want to make changes and to set clear aims and objectives, identifying priorities and deciding on what you hope to achieve. Any project must seek to answer a real need within your community or surrounding area. It is also likely to be specific to your congregation and community; it is not advisable simply to copy ideas from elsewhere.

Undertaking a community audit and consulting with your community

An audit will help you identify the needs of your community and identify potential partners, whether individuals or other organisations. If there is a neighbourhood plan (community plan) or local strategy being developed in your area, ensure that the church participates, as it is an ideal opportunity to tell your community what you can offer. Find your own unique selling point. Don't set up in competition with existing facilities; rather, add to or complement existing services.

Consulting your own congregation and the wider community is crucial. No matter how brilliant your project is, it will probably not work if you haven't taken people along with you. Making changes to a worship space or introducing additional uses can challenge many people's expectations of what a church should look like. A major reordering will raise concerns, and many churches receive initial opposition from the wider community. Take time to listen, explain your vision and, where appropriate, revise your plans. It is important to maintain people's support by keeping them informed, so keep communicating. Funders will want to see that the community is involved throughout.

Defining and developing the project

To make your project become a reality, you will need to:

- form a team of people to take it forward.
- devise a structure to manage initial project development and long-term delivery.
- consider what changes, if any, may need to be made to the building.

Time spent researching and planning before the project starts is never wasted. Applying for grants can be onerous and time-consuming, but the process will be a lot easier if you have fully developed your vision and objectives, worked out an implementation plan, produced a budget and developed strong relationships with your partners.

Take the opportunity to review all your plans and list everything you might want to do, such as improving accessibility, heating and lighting, and becoming more energy-efficient. Bear in mind that you won't necessarily achieve everything at once and may have to do things in stages, but ensure that each part fits in with everything else.

Often, only minor changes are required to enable a church building to continue serving its congregation while also offering new services to the community. Think about starting small and trying things out before embarking on a major reordering project.

Working with others

A major project, such as a building programme or a new community venture, will require a range of skills and some entrepreneurial ability. You will find some of these skills within your congregation and the wider community, but others will need to be developed as you go along. Having a management group of church and community representatives will strengthen links between church and community. It will also ensure that the project is 'owned' by everybody.

Engage with and work with others and you will find that people and money usually follow. There are plenty of resources and funding for community projects in general and also for specific uses, such as community shops. You may also want to build partnerships and deliver a service with a provider who is experienced in that field.

Increasingly, churches are learning to access community funding and separating community enterprises from faith activities. Likewise, it has become more acceptable for churches to host secular activities and facilities and there is less resistance from funders in supporting this type of venture.

Balancing the need for change with heritage and liturgical considerations

Once you have decided what you want to do, assess the impact that any changes may have on the fabric and internal fittings of your church. Don't start with preconceived ideas. Every church is different and many factors will determine the final outcome: particular architectural features, special internal furnishings, your style of worship, specific community needs, the preferences of the congregation and local community, the current viability of the building and its congregation, and how much money you think you will be able to raise.

You cannot undertake any works in your church until you have obtained the relevant permissions, which may involve both church and secular planning authorities. Ensure you check with your relevant building advisers at diocesan, district, synod or national level and find out what you need.

You will be required to present good reasons, showing that your scheme is based on a sensitive understanding of the cultural significance of your church heritage and will minimise any harm to the special historic, architectural, archaeological and artistic merit of the building, its contents and setting. You will be required to complete:

- a Statement of Significance, which describes the significance of what you have and how the building has evolved over time.
- a Statement of Need, which is your opportunity to explain and justify your proposals to all interested parties, outlining the impact of the proposed changes and why they are regarded as necessary to assist the church in its worship and mission. Liturgical requirements will have to

be balanced alongside any proposals for the enhancement of the building and wider use by the community.

Consult with the relevant church authority that looks after buildings, and other statutory consultants, as early as possible. Their advice is free and they can alert you to likely concerns, give you advice on what is likely to be approved and suggest alternative solutions. They have expert knowledge of all aspects of the history, development and use of church buildings, liturgy and worship, architecture and archaeology. They will also know of any similar projects that you could learn from.

Fundraising

Devise a funding strategy, starting with church members and then the local community. Tell these groups how they will benefit from the project. External donors will want to see that both groups are behind the project. It is a good idea to set up a small subgroup to identify those funders whose criteria match the aims of your project and to complete the application forms.

The fundraisers should be fully involved in the project development group so that they understand all aspects of it. Likewise, they should provide regular feedback to the group as a whole, so that if the fundraising process is slow, with too many rejections from potential donors, the whole group can work together to see if a change of strategy is required.

It is essential to have a business plan. All major funders will want to see evidence that your project is financially achievable and viable in the long term. You must show you have identified a real need, actual users for the revamped building and a realistic plan for the future running of the project, including start-up costs, charging structure, hiring charges and so on. It sounds daunting, but you will need to have brought this information together to manage a successful project.

Choosing the right organisational structure

Choose the right organisational and legal structure to allow you to do what you want to do. Also think about the long-term structure you will need to manage your project once it is up and running. It may be sufficient to have a management committee that is part of the PCC. It might be beneficial to set up a separate company—for instance, if your project involves some form of trading. If you are working in partnership with others, it is essential to agree appropriate legal arrangements that define responsibilities and obligations. Increasingly, churches are considering other models—for example, setting up a social enterprise, which is a trading organisation with social and community objectives; any surplus revenue will be used to fulfil social purposes.

The Buckland Brewer community shop opened in 2012 in the Methodist church vestry. Buckland Brewer Community Shop Limited has been set up as an Industrial and Provident Society to provide the legal entity to manage the shop using a community co-operative model. Some of the funds were raised from a Community Shares scheme. This has the added benefit of making each shareholder a member of the cooperative and thus a long-term supporter.[27] More information and advice on social enterprise and other forms of community ownership can be obtained from the Plunkett Foundation.[28]

Sharing sacred and community space

Sharing space is not always easy, and, even for congregations who want to provide a venue for a variety of activities, the reality can be a bit of a shock. Some people may not understand the sacred aspect of the building or may appear to be showing insufficient respect.

If you have genuinely gone into a partnership with the wider community and asked for their views and financial contributions, you have to be very sure that your vision for the building encompasses the new ways in which the building will be used and by whom. A good solution can be to have open and clear hire or lease agreements that define what is appropriate and what is allowed.

One issue that is often not completely resolved is how to maintain a quiet space while other activities are taking place. The chancel might be identified as that space, or separate soundproofed spaces could be created for noisy activities, such as a toddlers' group or café. In some cases, though, for some of the time, that quiet space is lost.

Long-term sustainability

Many projects report positive outcomes, bringing benefits to the congregation, the community and the building. Those benefits might include:

- provision of a much-needed community facility
- an increase in footfall and income
- new people joining the congregation
- a renewed engagement between church and community
- increased community well-being
- an increase in the number of people who value the church and will help to maintain it

In Elsfield, near Oxford, a small village of 100 people with no previous community space, there is now a well-used Village Room at the west end of the church. The main church building remains the responsibility of the church council, but the Village Room is managed by a committee of church members and non-churchgoing residents who raise the funds to cover its running and maintenance costs.[29]

St John the Evangelist, Fernham, in Oxfordshire, is now both the parish church and the village hall. The whole building is managed under a 30-year repairing lease by the Fernham Village Trust, which has responsibility for routine maintenance. The PCC pays to hire it for services and other church activities, such as weddings and funerals. The lease states that the trust will pay 60 per cent of the cost of any necessary major works, while the PCC will contribute 40 per cent, reflecting the split between chancel and nave. The Fernham village website is also a joint initiative between church and community.[30]

After adaptation, some churches find that their new building is not being used as much as they had hoped and they need to learn how to market it more effectively. Others find that while income increases, more activities mean higher running costs and administrative workloads. Setting up and clearing up after different activities can also be time-consuming. Such issues need to be thought through in the initial project planning. Projects also need to be set up so that they are not reliant on one or two people only, becoming vulnerable if those people (including the church minister) leave.

More people crossing the threshold can provide more opportunities for mission, but this has to be done sensitively. Some churches express disappointment when their hope of a larger congregation does not necessarily come to pass. However, many of these projects have enabled the church to survive as a place of worship, which is able to offer local people a place for quiet reflection, an inspiring building and a community space. More detailed information is available on many matters discussed in this chapter, including arrangements for different denominations, via the ARC website.[31]

Resources

- Resources for Rural Places of Worship: a central hub of resources related to the use and adaptation of rural church buildings for a variety of community-related purposes. **www.germinate.net/go/buildings**
- Auditing or Profiling for Rural Churches and Communities: an Introduction. **www.germinate.net/go/profiling**
- The Diocese of Hereford's (CofE) toolkit, *Crossing the Threshold: A community development approach to the use of church buildings*, is a step-by-step guide to developing and delivering sustainable community projects. **www.hereford. anglican.org/churchgoers/community_partnership_and_ funding/about_us_and_latest_news/index.aspx**
- ChurchCare provides guidance on making changes to the use or physical fabric of your church, as well as a guide entitled 'Improving the Visitor Experience'. **www.churchcare.co.uk**
- The Churches Conservation Trust's toolkit entitled 'Developing a Business Plan'. **www.visitchurches.org.uk/ regenerationtaskforce/Businessplantoolkit**
- The National Churches Trust provides guidance on all aspects of developing a church building. **www.nationalchurchestrust.org/building-advice**

- The Church of England's 'Parish Resources' offers twelve funding guides. **www.parishresources.org.uk/resources-for-treasurers/funding**
- Twenty-five case studies from Oxfordshire are described in *Churches for Communities: Adapting Oxfordshire's churches for wider use* by Becky Payne (Oxfordshire Historic Churches Trust, 2014).
- The Churches Visitor and Tourism Association's CD-ROM *Reflection on Church Tourism* provides guidance and case studies from across the UK. **www.cvta.org.uk**
- The National Churches Trust Resource Centre has links to a large cache of guidance on opening churches. **www.nationalchurchestrust.org/building-advice/resource-centre**
- Within the Methodist Church, Methodist Heritage aims to preserve and promote its heritage and use it as a tool for contemporary mission. **www.methodistheritage.org.uk**
- Many church tourism projects have produced valuable toolkits, including:
  - Divine Inspiration: **www.nationalchurchestrust.org/sites/default/files/resources/DI%20%28whole%29%20visitor%20welcome%20toolkit%202014.pdf**
  - The Northwest Multi-Faith Tourism Association's guide entitled 'Achieving Excellence in Visitor Welcome': **www.nationalchurchestrust.org/sites/default/files/resources/NWMFTA%20achieving%20excellence%20in%20visitor%20welcome%202012_0.pdf**
  - Inspired North East (Dioceses of Durham and Newcastle): **www.inspirednortheast.org.uk/page/useful-information/welcoming-visitors/1009**

- *Building on History: The Church in London* is a resource for researching the history of a church and producing education materials:
  www.open.ac.uk/Arts/building-on-history-project/index.html
- The guides, leaflets, trails and educational materials produced by the Southwell and Nottingham Open Churches Project offer good exemplars to follow:
  www.nottsopenchurches.org.uk
- The National Association of Decorative and Fine Arts Societies has designed Children's Church Trails, which can be adapted to suit your own church:
  www.nadfas.org.uk/what-we-do/nadfas-young-arts/church-trails
- The Heritage Lottery Fund offers funding for projects that aim to help people to learn about and engage with their heritage:
  www.hlf.org.uk/HowToApply/programmes/Pages/programmes.aspx#.U68FBPldVjY

Notes

1 Roger Munday, from the organisation Living Stones: www.living-stones.org.uk
2 See http://cvta.org.uk/wp-content/uploads/2014/11/cta_leaflet2012.pdf
3 Guidance Notes: Church Security, Ecclesiastical Insurance Group (2013). www.ecclesiastical.com/ChurchMatters/Images/PDF%20-%20church%20insurance%20guidance%20notes%20-%20security.pdf
4 www.ecclesiastical.com/churchmatters/churchguidance/churchsecurity/index.aspx;
www.ecclesiastical.com/churchmatters/churchguidance/churchsecurity/keeping-your-church-open/index.aspx;

Methodist Insurance: www.methodistinsurance.co.uk/
resources/church-guidance/church-security/index.aspx

5 www.ecclesiastical.com/ChurchMatters/Images/Personal%20
safety%20plan.pdf

6 www.germinate.net/go/opendoor

7 London Diocese offers guidance on installing glass doors:
www.london.anglican.org/kb/how-to-install-glass-doors-in-
your-church

8 Guidance on making disabled visitors welcome and
information on current legislation can be found via www.
churchcare.co.uk. See also English Heritage's publication, *Easy
Access to Historic Buildings* (2012): www.english-heritage.org.uk/
publications/easy-access-to-historic-buildings. The Centre for
Accessible Environments has guidance on undertaking an
access audit: www.cae.org.uk

9 www.stwulframs.org.uk

10 www.churchesfestival.info

11 www.hereford.anglican.org/churchgoers/welcoming_visitors_
and_tourists/index.aspx

12 www.visitherefordshirechurches.co.uk

13 www.discovershropshirechurches.co.uk

14 www.festivalofchurches.co.uk

15 http://saltaireurc.org.uk/visiting-the-church

16 The Church Guides website provides help for churches
wanting to improve their guidebook: www.churchguides.co.uk

17 www.fostd.org/default.aspx

18 'Crossing the Threshold: a community development approach
to the use of church buildings' (Hereford Diocese, 2013):
www.hereford.anglican.org/Content/Crossing%20the%20
Threshold%202013.pdf

19 Charles George, 'Shared Use of Church Buildings or Is Nothing
Sacred?' *Ecclesiastical Law Journal*, 6, 2002, pp. 306–317

20 See, for example, 'Building better neighbourhoods: the
contribution of faith communities to Oxfordshire life' (2010):
https://curve.coventry.ac.uk/open/items/32e0943c-358f-aed4-
b5ba-b65edb591304/1

21 www.germinate.net/go/trinitycreditunion
22 www.germinate.net/go/wickenbonhunt
23 www.spencerswoodchurch.org/meeting.htm#cafactive
24 www.germinate.net/go/bucklandbrewer
25 www.chalkevalleystores.co.uk
26 www.germinate.net/go/woldsvalley
27 http://bucklandbrewershop.com/?page_id=8
28 www.plunkett.co.uk
29 www.elsfield.net/church
30 www.fernham.info
31 Resources for Rural Places of Worship: www.germinate.net/
go/buildings

Bibliography

Mike Breen and Walt Kallestad, *A Passionate Life* (Kingsway, 2005)

W.J. Carter, *Team Spirituality* (Abingdon Press, 1997)

S.B. Ferguson and D.F. Wright, *New Dictionary of Theology* (IVP, 1988)

Sally Gaze, *Mission-Shaped and Rural* (Church House Publishing, 2006)

Paula Gooder, *Everyday God: The Spirit of the Ordinary* (Canterbury Press, 2012)

Robin Greenwood, *Being Church: The formation of Christian community* (SPCK, 2013)

David Heywood, *Reimagining Ministry* (SCM Press, 2011)

Louise J. Lawrence, *The Word in Place: Reading the New Testament in contemporary contexts* (SPCK, 2009)

J.M. Martineau, L.J. Francis and P. Francis, *Changing Rural Life: A Christian response to key rural issues* (Canterbury Press, 2004)

Sally Nash, Jo Pimlott and Paul Nash, *Skills for Collaborative Ministry* (SPCK, 2008)

Kathleen Norris, *The Cloister Walk* (Lion, 1999)

Martyn Percy and Louise Nelstrop, *Evaluating Fresh Expressions: Explorations in emerging church* (Canterbury Press, 2008)

J.A.T. Robinson, *The New Reformation* (SCM Press, 1965)

Anthony Russell, *The Country Parson* (SPCK, 1993)

Roger Standing, *Mosaic Evangelism: Sharing Jesus with a multi-faceted society* (Grove Books Ev102, 2013)

Bruce Stanley, *Forest Church* (Mystic Christ Press, 2013)

Robert Warren, *Developing Healthy Churches: Returning to the heart of mission and ministry* (Church House Publishing, 2012)

Messy Church Theology

Exploring the significance of Messy Church for the wider church

George Lings (ed.)

Messy Church Theology is the first title to encapsulate the theology of Messy Church. Through chapters by contributors from a variety of church and academic backgrounds and case studies by Messy Church practitioners, it gathers together some of the discussions around Messy Church and assesses the impact of this ministry, placing it in the context of wider developments within the church community.

Contributors include Lucy Moore, Steve Hollinghurst, John Drane, and Bishop Paul Bayes.

ISBN 978 0 85746 171 1   £9.99
Available from your local Christian bookshop or direct from BRF: please visit www.brfonline.org.uk

Outdoor Church

20 sessions to take church outside the building for children and families

Sally Welch

A creative worship and activity resource for churches to use outside the church building, Outdoor Church functions in any green space and is suitable for churches in urban, suburban and rural contexts.

- Four sessions for each season
- Four stand-alone service outlines, one for each season
- Material based on Bible stories and parables
- All-age activities and seasonal prayers
- Indoor alternatives for rainy days

ISBN 978 0 85746 416 3   £9.99
Available February 2016 from your local Christian bookshop or direct from BRF: please visit www.brfonline.org.uk

Also from BRF

Pioneering a New Future

A guide to shaping change
and changing the shape of church

Phil Potter

This book offers a map for pioneering a new future for the church. Writing as a pastor and practitioner, Phil Potter explains ways of shaping all kinds of change in the life of a church, particularly in the context of the many fresh expressions of church emerging.

Leaders can end up burnt out by their attempts to bring about change, while congregations are left damaged and disillusioned because they could not catch the vision. This is a book for leaders wanting to guide their Christian communities into a new future, and for church members wanting to be equipped for whatever lies ahead.

ISBN 978 0 85746 414 9   £7.99
Available from your local Christian bookshop or direct from BRF: please visit www.brfonline.org.uk

Enjoyed
this book?

Write a review—we'd love to hear what you think.
Email: reviews@brf.org.uk

Keep up to date—receive details of our new books as they happen.
Sign up for email news and select your interest groups at:
www.brfonline.org.uk/findoutmore/

Follow us on Twitter @brfonline

By post—to receive new title information by post (UK only), complete the form below and post to: BRF Mailing Lists, 15 The Chambers, Vineyard, Abingdon, Oxfordshire, OX14 3FE

Your Details
Name _____
Address_____
_____
Town/City _____ Post Code _____
Email _____

Your Interest Groups (*Please tick as appropriate)	
☐ Advent/Lent	☐ Messy Church
☐ Bible Reading & Study	☐ Pastoral
☐ Children's Books	☐ Prayer & Spirituality
☐ Discipleship	☐ Resources for Children's Church
☐ Leadership	☐ Resources for Schools

Support your local bookshop
Ask about their new title information schemes.